OFF THE BEATEN PATH IN BEIJING

北京自助游

Eleanor Liu

Foreign Languages Press

First Edition 2001

Edited by: Zhao You

Home Page:
http://www.flp.com.cn
E-mail Addresses:
info@flp.com.cn
sales@flp.com.cn

ISBN 7-119-02001-3

Published by Foreign Languages Press
24 Baiwanzhuang Road, Beijing 100037, China

Distributed by China International Book Trading Corporation
35 Chegongzhuang Xilu, Beijing 100044, China
P.O. Box 399, Beijing, China

Printed in the People's Republic of China

ACKNOWLEDGEMENTS

With special thanks to the following:

All members of the Tuesday Trotters, sometimes called Culture Club, Tuesday Group, Tuesday Tunnies or just the group, past and present.
John Liu, my husband
Kosima Weber Liu, my daughter-in-law
John D. Liu, my son
Michael Crook
Professor Wu Menglin
Professor Yu Qilong
Mr. Song Jinglun
Mrs. Lesley Walter
Mrs. Yu Ling
Mr. Bai Dacheng, his wife and son
Dr. Richard Hardiman
Professor Liu Deshan
Mr. Cui Yongping
Mrs. Wang Qiming
Liu Shuai
Professor Ding
Members of the Beijing International Society Committee
Guides and citizens who helped us locate various places

Eleanor Liu

TABLE OF CONTENTS

Preface

For many years I have been part of a small group whose makeup frequently changes (I have been the only constant member) dedicated to exploring in and around Beijing, looking for interesting places of all kinds which are not on the regular tourist routes. Hence the title of this book, "Off the Beaten Track in Beijing." Even on our visits to well known places such as Tiananmen Square and the Forbidden City we always managed to stumble on unusual and little-noticed features.

This ancient city is a treasure store of the quaint and the wonderful, sometimes just waiting around the corner. I have restricted myself to including only 94 locations in this book, but even this number will give you an idea of the scope for exploration. The descriptions and histories are not meant to be exhaustive, but are impressions and anecdotes which I feel touch on the essence of the places we discovered and make them come alive.

One of the greatest advantages and pleasures of living in Beijing, which is quickly becoming a cosmopolitan capital, is the opportunity to make friends with people from other countries and cultures. I now have friends all over the world from contacts I have made here.

The Tuesday Trotters, as we call ourselves from our habit of sallying forth on Tuesdays, choose our outings in many ways. We check the newspapers and special event notices in the hotels and tourist agencies. We also rely on our members for suggestions. We often meet someone who is interesting and arrange to take the group to meet them. Then one activity often suggests another as a follow-up. My teacher and friend, the artist Ye Xue has introduced us to several people and taken us to visit sites of historic importance. My son has introduced people who have invited us to visit them. Some places turn out to be disappointments. For instance, a carpet exhibition was advertised that promised to tell us all about the history of carpet weaving and the romance of colors, materials, etc., but it turned out to be no more than a sales room. However, we discovered other interesting places in the neighborhood and had a great lunch in a nearby restaurant, so the day was rescued.

Attempts to communicate between people whose languages and cultures are different can be frustrating–like the time we arrived at a friend's house for a swim party only to find that the gardener had thought that an instruction not to drain the pool had been the very opposite–but they can also result in chortles–like the time we ordered a cake for a farewell party for one of the Trotters, and it turned up bearing the message "Good Buy." There are also amusing mistranslations such as "confused nuts" for mixed nuts or "Silent Drawings" for "Still Life." We found a brochure that proclaimed "This is a great resort for vacating." At one time there was a tailor shop in Beijing with the sign "Ladies have fits upstairs."

A Chinese-speaking member of our group helped a visitor bargain with a vendor. After a considerable amount of haggling, a purchase was made, whereupon the vendor said in excellent English: "Thank you, ladies, it has been a pleasure doing business with you."

My life has been enriched by the friends I have made and the many fascinating things I have learned trotting around Beijing, and I look forward to many more adventures as well as many new friends.

I present this volume with the hope that it will encourage others to visit the places which gave me so much pleasure discovering in and around Beijing; I also hope it will encourage them to go out and explore on their own.

Eleanor Liu

Tiananmen Square: The Heart of Beijing
天安门广场：北京的中心

Tiananmen Square, the biggest public square in the world, covers 50 hectares, and measures 500 meters from east to west and 880 meters from north to south. It is the site of grand assemblies on occasions such as May 1, International Labor Day, and China's National Day on October 1.

In the center of the square is a flagpole, from which flutters the bright red national flag with five yellow stars. The red color signifies revolution, the big yellow star represents the Communist Party of China and the four smaller ones represent the Chinese people. This flag was first raised on October 1, 1949 by Chairman Mao Zedong, when he declared the founding of the People's Republic of China from atop the Tiananmen rostrum, which dominates the square from the north. Since May 1, 1991, the flag has been raised every day at sunrise. At 5:30 am, a group of guards appear at Tiananmen Gate. There are three guards in front, the middle one carrying the flag. Behind them, a group of 32 guards and a military band march along the north-south axis of the Forbidden City and cross the Golden River Bridge. They enter Chang'an Boulevard and begin a parade pace. The band plays the National Anthem while the flag is raised as the sun rises. The exact time is shown on the face of an electric clock in the square. It is a spectacular ceremony for early risers.

The first large-scale memorial built in New China was the Monument to the People's Heroes. It faces Tiananmen (Gate of Heavenly Peace) and its rostrum, which is the main south gate of the Forbidden City. The northern facade has a gilded inscription "Eternal Glory to the People's Heroes" in Mao's calligraphy. The southern facade has a longer inscription, composed by Mao but in the calligraphy of the late Premier Zhou Enlai. It reads: "Eternal glory to the people's heroes who laid down their lives in the people's war of liberation and the people's revolution in the past three years. Eternal glory to the people's heroes who laid down their lives in the people's war of liberation and the people's revolution in the past 30 years. Eternal glory to the people's heroes who from 1840 laid down their lives in the many struggles against internal and external enemies, for national independence and the freedom and well-being of the people."

Around the square are several famous buildings – Tiananmen to the north, Qianmen (front gate) to the south, the Great Hall of the People to the west and the Museum

of the Chinese Revolution and the National Museum of Chinese History to the east. Apart from the Great Hall of the People, where state banquets and ceremonies are held, all these buildings may be visited for the price of admission. The Mao Zedong Memorial Hall, where the embalmed body of the founder of the People's Republic of China lies in state, stands in the southern part of the square. It may be visited by appointment.

On the front of the Tiananmen Gate and high above the crowds, hangs a huge portrait of Mao. The first portrait was put in place overnight on September 30, 1949, just before the declaration of the founding of New China. At first the portrait was hung only on National Day and Labor Day, for a total of 10 days a year. But it has been a permanent fixture since the Cultural Revolution (1966-76). The portrait is six meters high and 4.5 meters wide and weighs 1.5 tons. Made partly of fiberglass and reinforced plastic, it is the largest hand-made portrait in Asia.

The original stones used to pave the square were replaced later by light-red natural granite slabs from Yi County in nearby Hebei Province. Each slab measures 99.5 cm by 49.5 cm by 15 cm, and weighs 210 kg. Two lawns were also added, as part of the capital's greening campaign.

Some of the original paving stones were obtained by Li Yongtian, deputy secretary general of the China National History Society, who commissioned a company to cut them into pieces measuring 120 mm by 50 mm by 96 mm. These dimensions reflect China's 1.2 billion people, New China's 50 years of history and the country's 9.6 million sq km of land area. Another set of the stones measures 120 mm by 21 mm by 96 mm; the 21mm symbolizes the wish for a bright 21st century for the Chinese people. The bricks are packaged in silk boxes. The stone numbered 491001 has been donated to the Museum of the Chinese Revolution.

Tiananmen Square is a pleasant spot for visitors to saunter around on fine days, and a favorite venue for kite flyers.

How to get there:

4 Jingshan Qianjie, Dongcheng District.

东城区景山前街4号。

The Forbidden City and the Palace Museum

故宫和故宫博物院

The Purple Palace constellation was thought to be the abode of the God of Heaven, so the emperors of ancient China, who claimed to be the "Sons of Heaven," named their residence "The Purple Palace." Because it was forbidden to the common people, it was also known as the Purple Forbidden City.

Construction of the Forbidden City in Beijing was begun in the fourth year of the reign of Emperor Yongle of the Ming Dynasty (1406), and was completed in the 18th year (1420). It was home to 24 Ming and Qing emperors over a period of more than 570 years.

It covers an area of 720,000 square meters, and houses one million rare and priceless relics collected by various monarchs. It is outstanding among the celebrated palaces in the world, having four times the floor space of the Louvre in Paris, more than twice that of the Kremlin in Moscow, more than ten times those of the Palace of Versailles and Buckingham Palace in London, and more than three times that of the Imperial Palace in Tokyo.

The number 9 figures prominently in the Forbidden City. The rooms number exactly 9,999; the nails on every door (except that of the East Flowery Gate) are arranged in 9 rows of 9 each. The East Flowery Gate has 8 rows of 9 to a row, but it is not known just why; some say it was the spirit gate through which the biers of deceased emperors were carried, so it had an even (*yin*) number. However, this gate was also used for other purposes. All the steps in the Forbidden City are in nines or multiples of nine. The ancients regarded nine as the largest numeral, a number to which only emperors were entitled. It also has the same sound as the Chinese word for "everlasting," so it symbolizes the emperor's wish that his reign would last forever.

The predominant color of the Forbidden City is yellow. According to the ancients, the universe is made up of five elements – metal, wood, water, fire and earth. Earth is the most basic of them all, and yellow, the color of earth, was almost exclusively used for emperors.

There is only one building in the Forbidden City with a roof of black tiles–the Wen Yuan Ge–the royal library. Black represents water, and water can overcome fire. Since fire was a constant danger to the book collection under the library's roof, the black tiles were a sort of "fire insurance."

All the buildings in the Imperial City are made of wood or brick. The wall circling the city contains 12 million bricks, each weighing 24 kilograms. High-quality bricks of a tawny color, polished and tightly fitted together, were used to pave the floors of the three main halls of the Inner Court. A special glue made from steamed glutinous rice and egg white was used to hold the bricks and stone slabs in place. Under this "gold brick" floor are furnaces and tunnels that supplied heat to the rooms on the left and right of the middle room, which opened to the outside. There were charcoal braziers in the main hall, used for heating in the winter. Charcoal was also used for cooking. There were no chimneys as such to let the charcoal smoke out, but openings for ventilation served the purpose.

Tens of thousands of huge stone slabs were used to construct the imperial compound. The largest lies behind the Hall of Preserving Harmony. Weighing 250 tons, it was hauled there during the Ming Dynasty some 50 km from Fangshan County, west of Beijing, by 20,000 laborers in the space of 28 days. It was done in winter, by making a road of ice, upon which log rollers were placed. Because the road had to be straight, any houses or other impediments in its way were demolished.

The stone has a border of spiraling grass carved in low relief. Its motif is nine dragons soaring among drifting clouds. The carving we see today is not the original one done in the Ming Dynasty; according to the records, in the 26th year of the reign of Qing Emperor Qianlong (1762), he ordered the

Board of Palace Affairs to have the carvings on the slab removed and a new design engraved on it to celebrate his mother's 70th birthday.

There is another stone carving of the same size on the front terrace of the Hall of Supreme Harmony. However, that one is made up of three slabs of different sizes pieced together. Records show that the carving on it was done in the Wanli reign period of the Ming Dynasty (16th century), when the "Three Great Halls" were being erected.

One of these halls is the Hall of Supreme Harmony, which was the venue for important court ceremonies, such as the rites of enthronement, and celebrations of imperial birthdays and royal weddings. To show the absolute authority and divine power of the emperor, dragon designs of superb craftsmanship adorn the hall from top to bottom. On the roof, the beams and rafters, the ceiling–everywhere there are countless dragons paying homage to the Son of Heaven.

Below the vaulted ceiling, the mid-section of which is decorated with flocks of dragons, there is a gold-lacquered throne carved in openwork and also bearing dragon designs, with a screen, both on a dais that descends to the floor level by a flight of seven steps. The back and armrests of the throne are engraved with dragons and the seat rests on an I-shaped pedestal. There is a total of 408 dragons on the throne, on the screen and the ornaments on and around the dais.

In fact, a rough estimate puts the total number of dragons painted, incised or carved in the interior and exterior of the Hall of Supreme Harmony at 13,844–flying, coiling or twisting, and all resplendently signifying the divine power of the emperor.

One cannot visit the Forbidden City without being impressed by the grandeur of the bygone imperial days of the Chinese Empire, and by the superb skill of the workers and artisans who built this magnificent palace complex.

How to get there:

4 Jingshan Qianjie, Dongcheng District.

东城区景山前街4号。

The National Museum of Chinese History

中国历史博物馆

This museum is particularly interesting for its collections of very ancient objects peculiar to China. In 1992, it held an exhibition of items unearthed from the tomb of Fu Hao, a woman general and ruler of the Shang Dynasty (c. 16th-11th centuries B.C.). Her tomb, excavated in 1976, yielded a wealth of bronze and jade articles. One jade figure was carved in the likeness of a woman on one side and of a man on the other.

Oracle bones are animal bones, antlers or tortoise shells which were used for divination purposes in remote antiquity. Holes were drilled in them, and they were heated over a fire until cracks appeared. The cracks were then "read" by shamans, as divine messages. The origin of Chinese writing has been traced back to the oracle bones.

The Western Zhou Dynasty (11th century-771 B.C.) was the heyday of bronze casting in China. Among the many bronze objects on display in the museum is the Guoji Zibai Tub. A gift from an emperor to General Ji Zibai, it was lost for 3,000 years, until it was dug up by a farmer in the early 19th century. It was later acquired by General Liu Mingchuan in 1864, who admired its exquisite decorative patterns. Liu built a pavilion around it, and later wrote a book about it. He prized it so much that when Emperor Guangxu wanted to buy it, Liu buried the tub once more. It was presented to the state by Liu's descendents after the founding of New China in 1949.

During the Zhou Dynasty, huge bronze vessels were used for ritual purposes, but also served as national archives, bearing lengthy inscriptions detailing the accomplishments of rulers, statesmen and generals. There were two methods of casting bronze – using sand or wax molds. The more unwieldy protruding decorations parts were cast separately and attached to the main body.

How to get there:

East of the Tiananmen Square, Dongcheng District.

东城区天安门广场东侧。

The Museum of the Chinese Revolution

中国革命博物馆

Sometimes the Museum of the Chinese Revolution, in Tiananmen Square, stages exhibitions which have nothing to do with revolution. One of these, which we visited in June 1992, was a collection of 4,000 precious stones. These ancient treasures were from the Forbidden City, Chinese Geology Museum, Beijing Museum of Natural History, Rongbaozhai Paintings and Antiques Emporium and personal collections from all over China.

The smallest stone was almost as big as an egg, while the largest was shaped like a stalactite and was over four meters high. The most precious stone was worth over two million yuan. Some of the stones had been specially polished to bring out the colors and markings.

Some of the exhibits were for sale, and some of our group succumbed to the temptation of these superb and rare objects for which the Chinese have such a fascination.

In August the same year, we returned to view a private collection of Rain Flower Pebbles. These unusual natural stones were tastefully arranged according to their natural patterns and shapes – flowers, animals, people, and even the four seasons. Some were arranged to illustrate a poem or legend.

The owner of the collection, Liu Shuai, was there, and he explained that Rain Flower Pebbles are found mainly in the region of his hometown, Nanjing. Legend has it that while a Buddhist monk of the Liang Dynasty (502-557) named Yun Guang was preaching, his discourse so pleased Heaven that it sent down a shower of flowers. The flowers then turned into pebbles of pleasing shapes and colors, hence the name. The more prosaic explanation of their origin is that they are the product of eons of friction in the jumbled waters of the Yangtze River. They may be classified into crystal, agate, jasper and quartz.

How to get there:

East of the Tiananmen Square, Dongcheng District.

东城区天安门广场东侧。

The People's Park
人民公园

This park used to be part of the Forbidden City, and the Working People's Cultural Palace inside it was the Shrine of the Imperial Ancestors. The architecture of this building is striking, with its huge beams and skillfully fitted brackets and eaves. Dragon carvings on some of the steps attest to its imperial status.

It is common to see art students painting pictures of the ancient cedar trees in the park, which often hosts exhibitions and performances. We visited an exhibition of handicrafts from India here. On display were gorgeous batik wall hangings, and items woven from straw, fabrics and thin wooden strips. In addition, there were bronze, gold and silver items, as well as musical instruments.

In September 1998, Puccini's Turandot was staged here, a tribute to the magnificent setting of the park. This version was directed by leading Chinese film director Zhang Yimou.

How to get there:

East of the Tiananmen Square, Dongcheng District.

东城区天安门广场东侧。

The China National Art Gallery

中国美术馆

The China National Art Gallery, or Meishuguan, is one of the largest of its kind in the country. When you enter, there are large galleries to the left and right, and in the center after ascending a short flight of stairs there is the Round Gallery, a very large room where special exhibitions are held.

In December 1999, there was an exhibition of prize-winning art consisting of 588 works. The works of the gold medal winners were displayed in the Round Gallery. This exhibition was the largest ever held by the Ministry of Culture.

We have visited the museum many times to view showings of art works by not only Chinese artists but also by artists from many other countries. In September 1995, there was a special showing of portraits painted by Wang Haiyan of exceptional women of the world. The show was mounted specially for the UN's Fourth World Conference on Women, held in Beijing. We were there when she presented a larger-than-life portrait as a birthday gift to Gertrude Mongella, the secretary-general of the Conference. There are shops with books, cards, art supplies and souvenirs for sale.

How to get there:

1 Wusi Dajie, Dongcheng District.

东城区五四大街1号。

The Wan Fung Art Gallery

云峰画苑

The gallery occupies two old buildings in the Beijing Archives Complex. It is a regular venue for art exhibitions both domestic and overseas.

In September 1995, we visited a show of about 40 works by artists from China, Australia and the US. On April 30, 1996, we were there again, for an exhibition by Dorrit Yacoby, an Israeli artist who follows the tradition of assemblage (layering of materials). Her works are allegories for mental states. In October 1998, we viewed an exhibition of masterpieces by Ehr Deke, the Shanghai photographer whose work illustrates the books by Tess Johnston mainly on Western architecture in China.

The main archives building has impressive red doors and intricately carved roof eaves. Once in the early 1980s, our group was allowed into the main building and shown the archive collections, including some displays of ancient records under glass. But it seems to have been closed to the public since then.

How to get there:

36 Nanchizi Dajie, Dongcheng District.

东城区南池子大街36号。

The Confucius Temple

孔庙

The Confucius Temple is located on Chengxian Street, in the northeastern part of the city. It was built in 1306, and is the second-biggest temple to the sage in China, next only to the one in Qufu, Confucius' birthplace in Shandong Province. This street is one of the few left in Beijing that still have decorated arches.

In front of the main hall, the Dacheng Hall are the Late Teacher's Gate and the Dacheng Gate. Dacheng means "a collection of all the good things," and is an expression often used in connection with Confucius. The Dacheng Hall has double flying eaves, crimson walls and a yellow roof. It stands on a white marble terrace, much like an imperial palace. Behind the Dacheng Hall is the Congsheng Shrine, in which the tablets of the ancestors of the Kong (Confucius' family name) are worshipped. Other buildings are Divine Kitchen, Well Pavilion, Sacrificial Pavilion, Fasting Room and Divine Store.

In the temple grounds are a number of large cypress trees, some of them 500 years old. A folk tale relates how when Yan Song, the wicked prime minister of Emperor Jiajing of the Ming Dynasty paid an official visit to the temple a branch of a cypress tree brushed his hat from his head. Later, when Yan Song was dismissed from office, the local people named the tree "The Tree Which Expels Evil."

There are more than 400 stone tablets preserved in the temple, 198 of which bear the names of successful candidates in the imperial examinations. Fourteen record meritorious deeds and events, and two are inscribed stone drums. In addition, there are 190 steles on which are carved 13 volumes of classical writings. They are known as the "Stone Classics of Qianlong." Traditionally ceremonies were held at the temple three times every year to honor Confucius. Nowadays only his birthday celebration is held.

How to get there:

Chengxian Street, Dongcheng District.

东城区成贤街。

The Dongsi Mosque

东四清真寺

Our group of seven was at first refused entrance to this mosque, so it seems that, unlike the Ox Street Mosque, they are not used to visitors. However, a young imam took pity on us, and guided us around.

The mosque was first built in 1447. A Middle Eastern-style minaret was added in 1486, but it collapsed during an earthquake in 1908. Only the dome-shaped top remains, with "cast in 1486" carved on the inside. As a result, the buildings all look Chinese from the outside.

The main prayer hall is made entirely of wood. The Repository Hall behind it is a beamless building, the supporting walls of which bear varicolored motifs and are in the Ming style. On the inside of the dome-shaped roof are painted verses from the Koran. The dome itself is not visible from the outside.

This mosque was protected by the late Premier Zhou Enlai from damage during the "cultural revolution." When we visited it in 1993, it had six resident imams.

How to get there:

Dongsinan Dajie, Dongcheng District.

东城区东四南大街。

The Russian Embassy

俄罗斯联邦大使馆

Covering 16 hectares, this compound is the largest Russian embassy in the world. Its origin dates back to 1658, when, following clashes between Chinese and Russian troops on the Amur River, 45 Cossacks and their wives settled in Beijing. They were formed into a special company under a Manchu Banner, or military division, by

Emperor Kangxi. As Bannermen, they were included in the second-highest class of the nobility in China at that time, and their rank was hereditary.

A small Buddhist prayer house was assigned for them to practice their Orthodox faith, and was named the Nikolskii Church. This became the site of the Russian Orthodox Mission, and for all practical purposes was for a long time the first foreign embassy in Beijing. A report to Peter the Great from a merchant described the newly consecrated church as being "on the right-hand side at the corner of the city, close to the wall, and next to the church is laid out a suburb for Russians dwelling in the Chinese capital."

Minister-Counselor Anton Vassiliev was our guide in May 1994. He told us that 20 missions, each residing in Beijing for about ten years were sent by the Orthodox Church to China. Treaties in 1689 and 1727 promoted the expansion of trade and cultural contacts between China and Russia. An additional site south of the original one was given to the mission. This is known as the Nanguan, the other being known as the Beiguan.

Following Napoleon's invasion of Russia in 1812, all contact with the homeland was lost. The mission members had to survive by their own efforts and small allowances from the Chinese government. But by 1860, the Legation Quarter had been established, with the influx of diplomatic missions from several other countries. The Nanguan became the site of the Russian Embassy, by "Soviet Embassy Compound Lane." The Beiguan was reserved for the Russian Orthodox priests. The Beiguan was sacked by the Boxers in 1900, and its famous library was destroyed. The priests had to take refuge in the embassy building.

The Soviet Union was the first foreign country to recognize the People's Republic of China in 1949. The empty Beiguan was allocated for the new mission, and redesigned by the architect who had designed Moscow University.

Mr Vassiliev showed us a stone clearly marked in cyrillic letters "Beijing Orthodox Mission," which had been unearthed during maintenance work only three days before our visit. In the palatial reception hall of the main building hang dazzling Bohemian crystal chandeliers, purchased in the 1950s and now priceless.

Outside, we strolled to a Chinese-style building known as the Red Mansion, modeled on an earlier building Emperor Kangxi had given the Russians. Inside is a tall antique screen made of ivory-inlaid wood, the most valuable piece of furniture owned by the embassy. We then walked by a splashing fountain, a canal and a sparkling pond. Russians love to live beside water, the minister-counselor's wife told us. Passing the children's playground, we came to a small Chinese pavilion on the spot where long ago the first Orthodox mission had been set up.

How to get there:

4 Beizhong Street Dongzhimennei, Dongcheng District.

东城区东直门内北中街4号。

St. Michael's Church

东交民巷天主堂

This Catholic church is located in the old Legation Quarter. It was built in 1902 as the French Embassy church. It had its first Chinese parish priest in 1952. Closed in 1958, it re-opened on Dec. 23 1989.

St. Michael's Church is worth visiting for its beautiful stained-glass windows.

How to get there:

Jia 13 Dongjiaominxiang, Dongcheng District.

东城区东交民巷甲13号。

St. Joseph's Cathedral

王府井教堂

This Catholic church stands on the site of one built by Louis Buglio in 1655, under the supervision of the Jesuit Fr. Verbiest, who had succeeded Adam Schall as minister of astronomy at the imperial court. The library of the church burned down in 1814, and Emperor Jiaqing seized the opportunity to have the whole church razed and the land confiscated. It was later rebuilt, but was destroyed by the Boxers in 1900.

The present structure, also known as the Dongtang or Eastern Cathedral, was erected by the French in 1905. Adjoining it is a school, still called the Catholic school. In June 1988, I was taken on a tour of the cathedral after giving a talk to the students of an English class at the school.

How to get there:

74 Wangfujing Dajie, Dongcheng District.

东城区王府井大街74号。

Some Old Temple Sites

寺庙遗址

One Tuesday in 1993, we went to track down the sites of several temples which had once functioned in the vicinity of the Forbidden City. We had found the names and locations in old records.

The Mahakala Miao, or Pudu Si, is now a kindergarten. When we told one of the teachers that most of us were also teachers, we were given a tour of the place, and saw that the carvings and roof eaves were still intact, and the main building still has the original large wooden pillars.

Another temple, the Baichi Si is also now a school, but we were not allowed to go inside. The site of the Zhouxian Miao is a school too, and there is little of the original temple remaining.

We had better luck at the Xuanren Miao, where we were not only shown around but were also allowed to take pictures. This site is now occupied by private residences, but the drum and bell towers, covered in vines, are still there and there is the base of what once was a stele, in the traditional shape of a turtle. The Xuanren Miao had been a clinic for acupuncture and moxibustion in the 1980s, but we saw no signs of this.

The site of the Wanshou Xinglong Si, which was founded at the order of Emperor Kangxi, is also occupied by residences. The people there were very friendly, and were eager to point out old bits of carvings, tiles and paintings.

Our last stop was the gate of what was once the Fuyou Si, leading to what is now the Tibetan Guesthouse. We were not allowed to enter, but had to be content with peering at the newly painted archway inside, with much red, blue and green, and golden dragons.

How to get there:

Dongcheng District.

东城区。

The Former Residence of Mao Dun

茅盾故居

Mao Dun (1896-1981) was one of the great literary figures of modern China. He was the author of *Midnight*, *Rainbow* and *Spring Silkworms*, representative novels of the Realist tradition. He also translated famous works from foreign languages, and engaged in a wide range of other literary activities.

Mao Dun's original name was Shen Dehong, and he was a native of Dongxiang in Zhejiang Province. He spent the last eight years of his life in a large Beijing courtyard house, with 20 rooms altogether and one courtyard each in the front and back of the house. Grapevines creep along a large trellis, two white wax trees and two cypresses guard happy memories and present a calm atmosphere in contrast to the nearby bustling Annei Dajie Street. In the center of the front courtyard stands a marble half-length statue of Mao Dun, erected in 1986. The back courtyard and its surrounding rooms remain as they were originally. In the sitting room there are rows of bookshelves preserved as they were when Mao Dun used them. The calendar on the big desk shows February 19, 1981, the day before he was hospitalized. A well patched set of night clothes hangs on one wall.

In his later years, Mao Dun contributed all the payments he received for his works, a total of 250,000 yuan (about US $30,120) to set up the Mao Dun Literary Award to encourage the production of novels.

How to get there:

13 Houyuan'ensi Street, Jiaodaokou, Dongcheng District.

东城区交道口后圆恩寺街13号。

The Fire God Temple

火神庙

In former times there were several temples to the Fire God in Beijing. We tracked one down in Andingmen St., not too far from the Drum Tower.

The entrance, with a small archway, is still intact, but the buildings have been turned into residences. The roof tiles and architectural style of the larger buildings identify the place as the site of a temple.

The residents were very friendly, and allowed us to wander about and take pictures.

How to get there:

Andingmen Dajie, Dongcheng District.

东城区安定门大街。

The Zhihua Temple

智化寺

This temple was built by the powerful eunuch Wang Zhen in 1443, as his family shrine. He introduced ancient court music to the temple, where it gradually fused with traditional Buddhist music and became the "capital music of the Zhihua Temple."

Six years after it was built, Wang Zhen was executed, and the temple was taken over by the imperial court.

It comprises three courtyards. There are seven halls in the front compound; the middle compound has the Tathagata Buddha Hall; and the rear compound has the Dabei and 10,000 Buddhas halls.

The Zhihua Temple's greatest treasure are the wooden blocks used for printing the Grand Collection of Buddhist Scriptures. Made during the Ming Dynasty, they are the only officially carved blocks of the scriptures in the Chinese language. Because they were made by imperial decree, they are called the Dragon Scriptures.

How to get there:

In Lumicang, Dongcheng District.

东城区禄米仓。

The Yonghegong Lamasery

雍和宫

The Yonghegong, or Palace of Harmony and Peace, was originally built by order of Emperor Kangxi in 1694. It was the residence of his son, who lived there until his ascension to the throne as Emperor Yongzheng. The rule was that a former imperial residence could not revert to secular use, so it was renamed the Yonghegong and declared a lama temple. Emperor Yongzheng's coffin was placed here when he died in 1735.

His successor, Emperor Qianlong, upgraded it to the status of an imperial palace, and its green tiles were replaced by ones of imperial yellow. Its principal components are three exquisite memorial archways and five major halls, all on a north-south axis. A long forecourt beyond a glazed tile arch leads to the first main courtyard, containing two stele pavilions, drum and bell towers and two fine bronze lions from the Qianlong period. At the rear is the Devaraja Hall, formerly the entrance to Yongzheng's residence. Immediately behind the hall is a bronze ding (tripod with a dark lustrous patina). Around the top are six pairs of dragons each playing with a pearl, and at its base are three lions playing with a ball, all very skilfully carved.

Beyond the ding is the square Yubiting (Pavilion of the Imperial Writing-Brush) with curved eaves and a double roof. It contains a stele inscribed in the Han, Manchu, Mongolian and Tibetan languages, explaining the significance and origin of Lamaism. Other halls are the Yonghedian (Hall of Harmony and Peace), Yongyoudian (Hall of Everlasting Protection) and the Falundian, Hall of the Wheel of the Law, which is seven bays wide. The final hall is the Wanfuge (Pavilion of Ten Thousand Happinesses), also known as the Tower of the Great Buddha. It is the tallest of the buildings in the Yonghegong. The central tower is three stories high, and is linked to the two-storied pavilions on either side by flying galleries.

In the middle of the temple stands a statue of Maitreya Buddha, which towers 18 meters above ground and descends eight meters below ground. This statue is carved

from a single trunk of white sandalwood, eight meters in diameter, which was a gift to Emperor Qianlong from the Seventh Dalai Lama. It was brought all the way from Tibet. It is said that when the statue was first installed it was fitted with a yellow monk's robe made of more than 1,800 meters of satin.

The Yonghegong also has a number of auxiliary buildings lining the courtyards on the east and west. Some of these display exotic Lamaist sculptures and paintings. The calligraphy of Qing emperors written on scrolls or inscribed on steles is also preserved.

How to get there:

12 Yonghegong Dajie, Dongcheng District.

东城区雍和宫大街 12 号。

Old Observatory

北京古观象台

Also called the Terrace of Ancient Astronomical Instruments, this observatory was built in 1279, during the Yuan Dynasty. It was the work of Guo Shoujing, a noted astronomer, hydraulic engineer and mathematician. It was opened to the public as a museum in 1956.

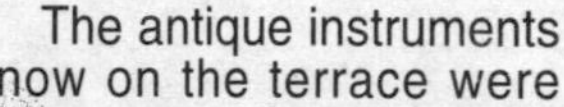

The antique instruments now on the terrace were constructed in 1674 by the Jesuit Ferdinand Verbiest at the behest of Emperor Kangxi. They consist of a quadrant, celestial globe, altazimuth, ecliptic armilla, sextant and zodiacal armilla. After the Boxer Movement of 1900, the Germans removed most of the instruments to Germany, where they were exhibited in a park in Potsdam. They were returned to China after World War I. There were originally 15 instruments, but seven were moved to Nanjing in 1931, and are on display at the Purple Mountain Observatory.

Emperor Kangxi appointed Verbiest president of the Board of Astronomy to assist in reforming the calendar. The emperor's respect for Western science had been imparted to him by his tutor (and Verbiest's predecessor) Fr. Adam Schall.

The terrace also houses exhibits and portraits pertaining to Matteo Ricci (1552-1610), another Jesuit and man of science who had great influence at the imperial court, Schall and Verbiest, acknowledging their and other Europeans' contributions to astronomy in China.

How to get there:

2 Biaobei Hutong Jianguomennei Dajie, Dongcheng District.

东城区建国门内大街裱褙胡同2号。

Zhongshan Park

中山公园

This is a lovely park on the west side of the Forbidden City. It is named after Sun Yat-sen. The flowers, trees and rock formations are beautiful, and are often changed according to the seasons. Gnarled cedar and pine trees shade the walkways.

The park is the site of frequent exhibitions. We have visited tulip, lotus, chrysanthemum and exotic rock displays. In 1992, we toured the Hall of Chinese Idioms here, where we saw ten groups of life-sized animated figures illustrating different Chinese expressions.

We also visited an underground gallery where figures of emperors from some 5,000 years ago right up to Pu Yi, the last emperor, and including Empress Dowager Ci Xi, were on display.

There was a spectacular lantern display in June 1992, with lanterns of all shapes and sizes in every corner of the park. In addition, there were displays of scenes from the classical novel *A Dream of Red Mansions*, as well as from Peking Opera and stories of the Eight Immortals, and statues of Guan Yin, the Goddess of Mercy. Inside one of the buildings were large lanterns shaped like boats, flowers and animals. When such shows are on, there are food stalls scattered here and there, doing a thriving business.

How to get there:

West of Tiananmen.

天安门西侧。

Jingshan Park

景山公园

Jingshan Park is the hill located on the meridian line north of the Palace Museum. It is also called Coal Hill, because coal for the imperial palace was stored at its foot at one time.

It was a small grassy hillock, known as Green Hill, when the Yuan Dynasty established its capital, Dadu, in what is now Beijing. The hill was enlarged by dumping mud dredged from surrounding lakes and moats on it. Then when the Ming emperors rebuilt the city the earth excavated to form the moat around the Forbidden City was piled there to form the present dimensions of Jingshan Hill. The name Jingshan means "prospect," and the hill was used exclusively as a pleasure park by the imperial families, who used to enjoy the cool breezes and panorama of the capital from there. The hill was opened to the public in 1928, and after 1949 it became a public park.

During the reign of Emperor Qianlong (1736-1796) of the Qing Dynasty, a palace was built on the north face of the hill, a glazed-tile pavilion was built on the peak and four other pavilions were constructed on the four other high points. For a time, the hill was called the Garden of a Hundred Fruits, because of the numerous fruit trees planted there. A later name was Longevity Hill.

The topmost pavilion – Wanchunting (Ten Thousand Springtimes) – was the highest spot in Beijing during the Qing Dynasty. Formerly, each of the pavilions contained a bronze statue of a god, which were collectively known as the Wuweishen (Five Flavor Gods). During the Boxer Movement of 1900, four of the statues were stolen by the forces of the Eight Allied Powers; the fifth suffered the loss of his left arm, but this was repaired later.

From the top peak, the southward view reveals the symmetrical plan of Beijing, with the ancient capital's buildings lined up along a central north-south axis.

On the eastern slope of the hill there once stood an old locust tree, or Chinese scholartree. On March 19, 1644, the last Ming emperor, Zhu Youjian, hanged himself from this tree as a peasant army led by Li Zicheng sacked the capital and put the Forbidden City to the torch. Another tree was planted to mark the site. There was once a stone stele there, bearing the words, "The place where the Ming Sizong (Zhu's posthumous title) emperor died for his country." In the 1950s the stele was replaced with a wooden plaque reading, "The place where the Ming Emperor Chongzhen (Zhu's reign period title) hanged himself."

On the north face of the hill is the Longevity of the Emperors Hall, which originally contained a collection of portraits of Qing emperors. These were removed later. In the 1950s, this hall was turned into the Beijing Children's Palace, a recreational and educational facility for the capital's young people.

To the east is the Guandedian (View of Virtue Hall), used during the Ming Dynasty for archery practice, and during the Qing Dynasty as a temporary resting place for deceased emperors before their funerals.

At the foot of the hill, inside the south and main gate of the park is the Qiwanglou (Superb View Tower). In the reign of Emperor Qianlong, officials and scholars used to pay their respects to a memorial tablet dedicated to Confucius here. It now functions as a souvenir shop.

How to get there:

North of Jingshan Qianjie, Xicheng District.

西城区景山前街北侧。

Beihai Park

北海公园

Situated in the heart of the old part of Beijing, Beihai Park was a pleasure ground for emperors of the Liao, Jin, Yuan, Ming and Qing dynasties. It is one of the most exquisitely designed ancient parks in China. It has been a public park since 1915.

Beihai literally means "northern sea," and refers to the large lake which is its main feature. In the 11th century, the rulers of the Liao Dynasty stayed at the Jade Islet Palace here while visiting the suburbs of the capital, known as Yanjing at that time. During the succeeding Jin Dynasty, Beihai Lake and Qionghua Islet (the present site of the White Dagoba) were included in the grounds of the imperial villa.

Kublai Khan, the founder of the Yuan Dynasty constructed his new capital, Dadu, on the ashes of the Jin capital, with Beihai at the center. During the Ming and Qing dynasties, Beihai continued to be used as an imperial pleasure garden, and several large-scale construction projects were carried out there. The White Dagoba Temple (a dagoba is a dome-shaped Buddhist shrine containing sacred relics) was built on the island site of the Palace of the Moon, and the island was renamed White Dagoba Hill. The dagoba was badly damaged in an earthquake in 1679, and rebuilt the following year. Emperor Qianlong had several new structures built, including the Temple of Revealing Happiness, the Little Western Heaven, the Hall for Gazing at the Water and the Tranquil Heart Studio.

To the south of the Beihai Stadium stands the Jiulongbi, or Nine-Dragon Wall. Built in the Ming Dynasty, the wall is 6.9 meters high, 25.5 meters long and 1.4 meters thick. It is constructed entirely of glazed tiles. On each side, nine coiling dragons are depicted frolicking among waves and clouds.

Another unusual feature is the Tieyingbi, or Iron Screen, which stands in front of the Hall for Gazing at the Water. It derives its name from its color and texture, resembling iron ore. It is four meters wide and two meters high. It is decorated with mythical beasts, and is said to date from the Yuan Dynasty. The screen was formerly housed inside the bell-casting room at Deshengmen until it was moved for display at Beihai in 1947.

On the south bank of the lake is the Tuancheng (Round City), enclosed by a wall five meters high. It has a separate entrance outside the southern gate of Beihai. It was originally an island formed from the lake excavations in the 12th century. It now has an area of 4,500 square meters and is home to an 800-year-old pine tree. The main building in the Tuancheng is the Chengguangdian, or Hall to Receive the Light. The hall houses a statue of Buddha 1.5 meters high and carved from a single piece of lustrous white jade. The head and robes are inlaid with red and green precious stones. The statue is thought to have been brought from Myanmar in the late 19th century. The sword scar on the left arm is a relic of the intervention by the Eight Allied Powers during the Boxer Movement of 1900.

The Yuwanting, or Jade Bowl Pavilion, identifiable by its blue roof and white columns, stands in the middle of the Tuancheng. The jade bowl inside was used as a wine cup by Kublai Khan. It was later used by Taoist priests, with their typical disdain for worldly ostentation, as a pickle jar. It was recovered in 1749, and the pavilion built to protect it by order of Emperor Qianlong. It is carved from a single piece of black jade. It is decorated with images of sea dragons and other marine beasts sporting in the waves. Inside there is inscribed a poem about the bowl written by Emperor Qianlong.

How to get there:

1 Wenjin Street, Xicheng District.

西城区文津街1号。

Prince Gong's Garden

恭王府花园

This is one of the best examples of a traditional Chinese aristocratic garden surviving in Beijing. The garden and its surrounding mansion were built in 1777 by He Shen, a favorite of Emperor Qianlong. He Shen was notoriously corrupt, and after the death of his patron Qianlong's successor ordered him to commit suicide. The property then passed to a Manchu prince, and in 1851 to Prince Gong (1833-1898), who was an important shaper of Qing Dynasty foreign policy.

Special features of the garden are the Moon Viewing Pavilion and the Bat Hall, with its winged shape. Indeed, the bat motif recurs throughout the garden (the Chinese word for "bat"–*fu*–being a homonym for "good fortune"). The zig-zag paths and covered walks are laid out in complete harmony with the arrangements of hills, rockeries, flowers and trees.

Inside a cave made of a rockery there is a tablet bearing the character for "bat" upside down. The calligraphy is that of Emperor Kangxi. He gave the tablet to his mother when she was gravely ill. As she recovered soon afterwards, the tablet was greatly revered. How it got to Prince Gong's Garden is a mystery.

The small room to the right of the front entrance to the main building was the residence of the family tutor, who instructed the younger males. The small rooms on the other side were used by male guests or as studies. In the southwest corner of the compound is a courtyard, which was reserved for the male servants. According to the Chinese theory of geomancy, or "*feng shui*," the southwest corner was the most inauspicious part of the compound.

Typical of a mansion of this type, the buildings are divided into "*jian*," or bays. A "*jian*" is the space between pillars, and as there is always an even number of pillars, there is always an odd number of "*jian*." In former times, there were strict rules about the number of "*jian*" a residence could have; more than three presupposed a certain social status. There were also certain trees or plants which were barred from growing in the courtyards of the lowly, such as evergreen, pear and mulberry trees. Status was also indicated by different types of gates and their doors, and the number of "door hair pins," the rosettes above the doors, clearly showed the position and wealth of the owner. Stone drums, decorations above the gates, the width of the doors, and whether there were arches or pillars all indicated the status of the occupant. A later development was the "barbarian's gate," which was made by blocking the original wide gateway with a wooden wall, and piercing it with a small door, said to be in imitation of foreign practices.

How to get there:

Jia 14 Liuyin Street, Xicheng District.

西城区柳荫街甲14号。

Guo Moruo's Residence

郭沫若纪念馆

Guo Moruo (1892-1978) was a noted novelist, poet, historian and literary critic. He took part in the May Fourth Movement of 1919,and joined the Chinese Communist Party in 1927. After spending several years in Japan, he returned to China during the war against the Japanese invaders. He worked closely with Zhou Enlai, and held a number of important posts after the founding of the People's Republic of China.

His former residence has an interesting history. In the early Qing Dynasty, the land was a garden belonging to the notorious official He Shen. In the mid-19th century, it served as a straw storage and horse paddock for Prince Gong's nearby mansion. During the first half of the 20th century, the prince's descendants sold it to a leading pharmacy in the capital.

After 1949, it was the embassy of the Mongolian People's Republic, and then Soong Ching-ling, honorary chairman of the People's Republic of China, lived there for a short time. It was the home of Guo Moruo from 1963 till his death.

When my husband made a visit to China in 1973, he met and talked with Guo Moruo in his home. We also know his youngest daughter, and have attended parties and other events held in the residence.

The grounds are spacious and contain a double-courtyard house, which is preserved much the way Guo left it at his death. The buildings include his office and living quarters, his library and his wife's painting studio. An unusual feature is that several of the structures are connected by heated corridors, which was a luxury in Beijing in those days.

How to get there:

18 Qianhai Xijie, Xicheng District.

西城区前海西街18号。

The Former Residence of Soong Ching-ling

宋庆龄故居

Soong Ching-ling was the wife of Sun Yat-sen, the leader of the modern Chinese democratic revolution, and later honorary chairman of the People's Republic of China. Her former residence was a building renovated under the direction of the late Premier Zhou Enlai and presented to her in 1962.

It stands on a site which was owned by Prince Chun, the father of the last Qing emperor, Pu Yi. Prince Chun used it as a garden, but all the buildings in it had fallen into disrepair. The solidly built two-story house that Soong Ching-ling lived in is a combination of Western and Chinese architectural styles, with double-glazed windows and spacious rooms.

The house remains much as Soong left it, with her manual typewriter, library of English books, and tributes and gifts from all over the world. A bust of Soong stands before the entrance. There is a special exhibition hall divided into eight sections, highlighting different periods of her life, with numerous photographs, documents and other memorabilia, dating back to her childhood.

The garden is elegantly laid out, with rockeries and ponds, and planted with pines, cypresses and flowers. Halls and pavilions in traditional style are linked by winding corridors. Water from the nearby Houhai (Rear Lake) flows through an underground channel to form a stream.

How to get there:

46 Houhaibeiyan, Xicheng District.

西城区后海北沿 46 号。

The Old Beijing Library

国家图书馆分馆

The library has its origins in the Hall of Learning of the Imperial College (the Hanlin Academy). This was built in 1287, during the Yuan Dynasty, and was where the emperor would go occasionally to discuss the classics with court officials and students of the Imperial College. During the reign of Emperor Qianlong (1736-1796) of the Qing Dynasty, the building was greatly enlarged.

The main building was completed in 1931, when it became the Beijing Library. After renovation in the early 1950s, it was renamed the Capital Library, and a six-story building with storage capacity for 1,200,000 volumes was added.

The location, next to Beihai Park, is a pleasant one, and the grounds of the library are well tended, with hedges, rose bushes, grass and flowers. Before the main entrance there are statues of lions and elephants. Inside the main gate there are two wells and the Gate of Lofty Scholarship (Taixuemen). Further on, there is a memorial archway of glazed tiles with a bell tower and a drum tower to the east and west. Then there is the Jade Disc (Bigong) Hall. In the center of a circular pond stands a square pavilion, with a double-eaved roof topped by a gilded sphere. The pond has four stone spouts shaped like dragon heads, and the island–which was where the emperors held scholarly seminars–is reached by four marble bridges.

How to get there:

Wenjin Street, Xicheng District.

西城区文津街7号。

The Church of the Sacred Heart

西什库北堂

There are 15 Roman Catholic churches in Beijing –six in the city proper, and the rest in the suburbs. The Catholic population of the capital numbers about 40,000.

Also known as the North Church, the Church of the Sacred Heart is one of the four Catholic cathedrals in Beijing. It was built at the direction of a French priest in 1887. Badly damaged during the "cultural revolution," it has been restored, but unfortunately the old stained-glass windows are gone forever.

The grounds are well tended, with trees, flowers and grottoes. An elderly volunteer caretaker took us inside, and we found that the pillars were all painted bright red and green–quite a contrast to the pastel blue and white of the exterior. Our guide told us that the pillars had been blue, but the restorers had decided that glaring red and green looked more Chinese.

The church has two towers, with a bell in each. Our guide rang the one above the choir loft, but said that the one in the other tower is too heavy for one person to ring. There was formerly a pipe organ in the church, one of only three of its kind in the world (the others being in Paris and Shanghai), but it was dismantled during the "cultural revolution."

How to get there:

33 Xishiku Dajie Xi'anmen, Xicheng District.

西城区西安门西什库大街33号。

Liu Yin Folk-Custom Hutong Tour

柳荫街胡同游

It was the coldest day of the year when we toured the Liu Yin hutongs, near Beihai Park. First, we watched the Liu Yin Community dancers perform a traditional street dance. We then visited a home for elderly people of the neighborhood.

A highlight was an introduction to a bi-lingual kindergarten (Chinese and English), which seemed very well equipped and well managed. The children, aged from two to six, board at the school from Monday to Friday. It is more expensive than other kindergartens, but there are 60 pupils and a long waiting list.

We walked the short distance from there to Prince Gong's Mansion, and welcomed the opportunity to sit in the theater for a while to thaw out and drink hot tea, which one of the group had so thoughtfully brought in a thermos.

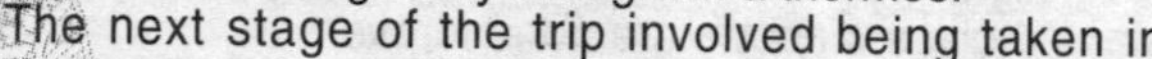

The next stage of the trip involved being taken in pedicabs, well wrapped up in lap robes. We were shown old alleys, traditional doorways and a courtyard house which was being renovated for sale, which was unusual as most of Beijing's courtyard houses are being torn down. At the Liu Yin Community Service Center we were told about the neighborhood by one of the pedicab drivers, who had grown up there.

How to get there:

Liuyin Street, Xicheng District.

西城区柳荫街。

The Temple of Great Charity

广济寺

This temple, the Guangjisi, houses the offices of the China Buddhist Association and the China Buddhism Research Institute. It was first built in the Jin Dynasty (1115-1234), and has been destroyed and rebuilt several times. In 1699 Emperor Kangxi ordered it renovated and expanded.

The worst disaster to overtake the Guangjisi occurred in 1934, when a fire destroyed invaluable manuscripts, and objects of porcelain, bronze and jade. A stone tablet engraved with a poem by Emperor Qianlong, "*Ode to the Iron Tree*," stands on the spot where an ancient tree once grew.

Inside the front gate is the Hall of the Heavenly Kings and the drum and bell towers. In the center of the compound is the Mahavira Hall (Daxiongbaodian). There is also the Hall of Perfection, which houses bronze images of the Goddess of Mercy and a collection of fine Buddhist paintings. The Daxiongbaodian has an unusual roof ridge, commonly called "Sea of the Fragrant World." Glazed tiles form a hill on the ridge, which bears designs of water, a lotus flower and a Sanskrit letter indicating "everlasting world."

In the Hall of the Heavenly King there is a statue of Maitreya Buddha cast during the Ming Dynasty. It has a kind and dignified expression, much different from the usual statues of this deity, which feature a huge belly and a beaming smile.

How to get there:

25 Fuchengmennei Dajie, Xisi, Xicheng District.

西城区西四阜成门内大街25号。

The Miaoying Temple

白塔寺

Also known as the Baitasi (White Pagoda Temple), this temple boasts the oldest Buddhist pagoda in Beijing. It was first built in the time of Kublai Khan (1215-1294), but was destroyed by fire toward the end of the Yuan Dynasty, although the pagoda survived. It got the name Miaoying when it was rebuilt in the Ming Dynasty.

There are four halls, standing in a line. Gifts from Emperor Qianlong for the renovation of the temple in 1753 are kept in the Hall of the Deva Kings. They were discovered during the repairation of the damage done to the temple by the Tangshan earthquake of 1976.

The pagoda, of a type known as a dagoba, distinguished by the top which is in the shape of an inverted alms bowl, stands in a courtyard in the rear part of the temple. It is a copy of a Nepalese style of pagoda, and was constructed under the supervision of a Nepalese engineer. The courtyard is reared two m above the outside ground. The dagoba is 50.9 m high. It consists of three parts: the base, the body and the crown. The base is nine m high, decorated with 24 lotus petals. The body is some 18.4 m in diameter, and shoulders the 13 concentric rings of the vault of Heaven. The rings are topped by a plate-shaped canopy, 9.7 m in diameter and made of hardwood covered with plain copper tiles. Hanging from the canopy are 36 strings of engraved copper tassels and bells. The crown of the pagoda is 4.2 m high, and weighs four tons.

The temple entrance was once difficult to find, because it had been blocked by houses and shops. But the area was cleared in 1998, improving access.

How to get there:

171 Fuchengmennei Dajie, Xicheng District.

西城区阜成门内大街171号。

The Lu Xun Museum

鲁迅博物馆

Lu Xun (1881-1936) was closely involved with many of the dramatic social changes which have occurred in modern China, and his writings strongly influenced the thinking of many Chinese both during and after his lifetime.

Chairman Mao Zedong once said, "Lu Xun was the bravest and most correct, the firmest, the most loyal, and the most ardent national hero, a hero without parallel in our history."

Lu Xun (real name Zhou Zuoren) bought a typical small Beijing courtyard house in 1923. He renovated it and installed in it his old furniture from his hometown Shaoxing, Zhejiang Province.

In the north wall of the main room, Lu Xun cut a door and connected to it a small room with a big window which let in lots of light. This room he called the "tiger tail" or his "green woods study." It served as both bedroom and study, and it was here that he wrote some of his most famous works, among them *Wild Grass*, *Dawn Blossom Plucked at Dusk*, *Wandering* and some of the essays in *The Grave*.

The desk that he wrote at still stands by the eastern wall, and on it are his inkstone, writing brush and kerosene lamp. The simple plank bed is testimony to Lu Xun's austere lifestyle.

The south room is a reception room and library, which houses a big set of bookcases designed by Lu Xun himself. They consist of an array of wooden boxes which can be dismantled for transportation.

To the east of the former residence is the Lu Xun Museum, which contains a comprehensive collection of his work. It has an affiliated research organization–The Institute of Lu Xun Studies–established in 1975. The two-story exhibition building contains 10,000 of Lu Xun's manuscripts, cultural relics he collected and other materials concerning his life.

How to get there:

19 Gongmenkou Ertiao, Fuchengmen, Xicheng District.

西城区阜成门宫门口二条19号。

The Portuguese Cemetery

利玛窦墓

This cemetery was part of property known as Shala, confiscated by imperial order from a eunuch named Yang and given to the Portuguese Mission of Beijing. Fr. Matteo Ricci, who founded and was the superior of the Mission, was the first to be buried there. Ricci was considered to be the most important European to work in China since Marco Polo, and was referred to as the "Wise Man from the West."

The Boxers desecrated the cemetery on June 17, 1900, opened the graves of the Christians and burned the bones. In 1903, the Marist Brothers bought five hectares of adjoining land, and doubled the area of Shala. A church was also built. Shala was restored as a cemetery, and in 1919 a teachers' training school and a primary school for neighborhood children were opened. The last Marist brothers left in 1954, and the Beijing Communist Party Training School was established at Shala in 1956.

The tombstones of Ricci, Schall and Verbiest were removed during the "cultural revolution," but returned in 1984, after Prof. Wu Menglin had been put in charge of the renovation of the cemetery in 1979. The city of Beijing placed a plaque at the entrance, explaining the historical significance of the site.

The tombstones contain much Chinese decoration, with inscriptions in Latin and Chinese on the front, and in the Manchu language on the back.

There is a separate yard housing 60 steles commemorating Jesuits from Italy, France, Portugal and other countries.

How to get there:

In Maweigou, Xicheng District.

西城区马尾沟。

The Former Memorial Temple to Prince Yi Xuan

奕譞墓

This temple was erected in 1891 to commemorate Prince Yi Xuan, a favorite of Empress Dowager Cixi, who granted his family the privilege of building it.

It has four halls covered with shining glazed tiles, one behind the other and all facing south. There are three courtyards containing smaller buildings nestling among ancient pine trees. The halls have iron or bronze vats on both sides of the doors, reminiscent of the Forbidden City.

There are stone tablets upon which are engraved stories of famous generals of former times in the yards, some lying under the trees and some used as tables. They were set up in 1939, when the government converted the temple into one honoring warriors in Chinese history. There were 40 tablets originally, but most are now missing.

There are two statues standing beside their pedestals since they were taken down by the Red Guards during the "cultural revolution." They are of General Guan Yu of the Three Kingdoms Period (220-280) and General Yue Fei of the Song Dynasty (960-1279).

One of the halls was the Beijing office and residence of the 14th Dalai Lama from 1951 to 1954. He moved to another residence in Dongjiao Minxiang, in the center of the city, and the temple hall was made into the representative office of the People's Government of the Tibet Autonomous Region. The Dalai Lama's former bedroom, meeting room and study are now offices, but there remains an exotic lamp hanging from the ceiling in the former bedroom, left behind when he moved out.

The lamps in the courtyard are in Tibetan style. They date from 1987, when the smaller halls were renovated and became the Qomolangma Hotel.

Although it is not officially open to tourists, the hotel guard will usually allow individuals to go in and have a look.

How to get there:

149 Gulouxi Dajie, Xicheng District.

西城区鼓楼西大街 149 号。

The Home of Mei Lanfang

梅兰芳纪念馆

The home of modern China's best-known Peking Opera actor was turned into a memorial museum in 1986. Mei Lanfang (1894-1961) specialized in female roles, and his house, where he lived from 1949 to 1961, is a typical Beijing courtyard dwelling covering 700 sq m. The inscription on the gate, "Mei Lanfang Memorial Museum," was written by Deng Xiaoping.

A marble bust of Mei is located inside the gate. His precious collection of books, manuscripts, works of calligraphy and paintings were donated to the museum by his family.

A verandah with red-lacquered pillars decorated with colorful drawings on the eaves joins the east and west wing rooms to the main rooms in the northern section. The northern rooms are Mei Lanfang's living room, study and bedroom, and all are furnished as they were in the artist's lifetime. Works of calligraphy and paintings presented to Mei by his artist friends hang on the walls. In the outer courtyard is an exhibition hall, which was formerly the reception room. It contains a pictorial record of Mei Lanfang's life and career.

How to get there:

9 Huguosi Street, Xicheng District.

西城区护国寺街9号。

The Xu Beihong Memorial Hall

徐悲鸿纪念馆

Xu Beihong (1895-1953) was an outstanding modern Chinese painter and art teacher. The memorial hall was originally located in his residence, but was moved to its present location when the house was demolished as part of Beijing's subway construction. His studio has been reconstructed just as it was when he worked in it.

Xu was particularly renowned for the way he could capture images of horses. As well as displays of his works, the new hall contains a pictorial summary of Xu's life and career. There are photographs of his visits to many countries, and his correspondence with schoolchildren, as well as telegrams of condolence upon his death from Chinese leaders.

How to get there:

53 Xinjiekoubei Dajie, Xicheng District.

西城区新街口北大街53号。

Deshengmen

德胜门

Deshengmen means "embrasured watchtower." It was built in the fourth year of the reign of Emperor Zhengtong of the Ming Dynasty (1440). As part of Beijing's city wall, it played an important role in the defense of the capital.

The renovated watchtower houses shops and an art gallery. One of the huge cannons which used to be stationed here is still located on its gun platform, which affords a panoramic view of Beijing.

How to get there:

On the west of the North Second Ring Road.

北二环路西路。

Rendinghu Park

人定湖公园

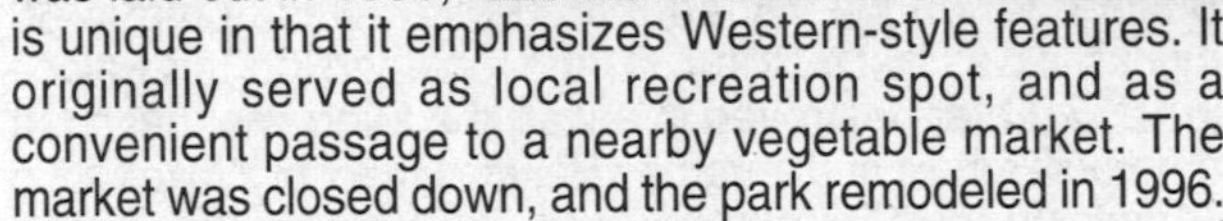

This park, which was laid out in 1958, is unique in that it emphasizes Western-style features. It originally served as local recreation spot, and as a convenient passage to a nearby vegetable market. The market was closed down, and the park remodeled in 1996.

The designer, Tan Xin, used the three salient features of Western parks–lawns, pools and statues–in a harmonious manner to give the park its Western flavor. There are no benches, but large black stones placed in the shade of trees form resting places. Six blue 20-m-high towers overshadow a man-made lake, which has an umbrella-shaped pavilion.

In the southern part of the park, varieties of Western building styles from different ages are represented. Zigzag walls enclose Greek, Roman and French courtyards, as well as a churchyard from the Middle Ages. The most outstanding construction is called River Sources. It is an Italian-style garden with a three-tiered fountain topped by three marble statues representing the mother rivers of three ancient civilizations. The statues along the main path in this area of the park are replicas of Roman and Greek masterpieces.

Tan Xin said that he wanted to provide a window on the gardens of the world for the local people.

We visited the park in 1997, and enjoyed the beautiful lawns and flowers. There are paved walks, and large open spaces for dancing or exercising. Very few people were out at that time–mostly grandparents with small children. However, there were two newlywed couples having pictures taken against a backdrop of Greek architecture.

How to get there:

In Deshengmenwai Dajie, Xicheng District.

西城区德胜门外大街。

The White Cloud Temple

白云观

This temple was until recently the only Taoist temple in Beijing. When we visited it in 1992, it was home to 60 monks. It was first built in 739, and renamed the Taiji Palace in 1203. Later destroyed in a war, the Ming imperial court ordered it rebuilt and renamed Baiyun Guan, or White Cloud Temple, in the 15th century.

The front gate is very impressive, having three openings representing the Three Worlds of Taoism–the World of Desire, the World of Substance and the World of Non-Substance. On the gate is an image of a monkey, which people touch for good luck as they enter. There are supposed to be three such monkeys altogether in the temple. We saw one other, but the whereabouts of the third is a mystery.

Outside the gate are decorative pillars and stone lions, and inside are flagpoles from which yellow flags bearing dragon patterns flutter. Further inside, there is a large wooden archway and an arched bridge with a bell hanging beneath it. People throw coins at the bell, which if struck is supposed to bestow blessings.

The Tutelary Deity Shrine was built in 1456, and renovated in 1662. The god enshrined there is Wang Shan, who has the onerous task of doling out all the good and evil in the world. On the walls are the portraits of his four marshals–Ma Sheng, Zhao Gongmin, Wen Qun and Yue Fei.

The Jade Emperor Shrine dates from 1662. The walls are decorated with depictions of the Six Southern Stars, the Seven Northern Stars, the 28 Star Deities and the 36 Celestial Kings–all features of the Taoist philosophy.

The Lao Lu (Old Way) Hall contains statues of the seven Taoists who achieved perfection. This hall was the site of ordination ceremonies during the Qing Dynasty.

In the temple grounds there is the bronze statue of a horse, said to represent Emperor Kangxi's warhorse. People with ailments touch the corresponding part of the horse in the hope of a cure. Interestingly, the shiniest parts of the horse are its knees, back and head.

A huge bowl made from gnarled tree roots was a present from Emperor Qianlong.

The Hall of the Four Guardians houses statues of the emperors of Heaven, Earth and the North and South Poles. In 1662 a pavilion was added for statues of the three most exalted gods of Taoism–Jade Purity, Upper Purity and Supreme Purity. In front of the hall is a bronze tripod cauldron. Cast in 1529, it is 1.16 meters high and it is decorated with 38 writhing dragons. Each of the three legs bears the head of a lion.

In one of the side buildings is a museum relating to this historic temple. The statue of Laozi, the founder of Taoism, in the museum was given to the temple in 739 by Emperor Xuanzong of the Tang Dynasty. It disappeared during the "cultural revolution" but was found again in 1979.

Among the curiosities in the museum is a small statue of a man riding a duck. It is said that this indignity was his punishment for plotting against his brother. Copies of this figurine can be seen decorating the roof eaves of old houses in Beijing. At the back of the temple complex is the Yunji Garden, which contains the Ordination Terrace. the temple ordains novices in spring and summer every year.

The temple has both bell and drum toworc, which waken the monks at 5:30 a.m. Among their many chores is that of guiding visitors around the temple; our guide spoke excellent English, and was most informative.

How to get there:

Binhe Road, Guang'anmen, Xicheng District.

西城区广安门滨河路。

The Lao She Teahouse

老舍茶馆

When Lao She wrote his famous play "Teahouse" in 1957, there were only few teahouses left in Beijing, where once they had been a street-corner fixture since the Song Dynasty (960-1279). In fact, the last one was closed down in the following year. However, in 1988 Yin Shengxi decided that it was time to revive the old tradition, and in December of that year the Lao She Teahouse opened for business on busy Qianmen street.

With a loan of 1,000 yuan (not much more than US$100 in those days), Yin bought some large teapots and 100 tea bowls to set up his business. The price of tea has remained at two *fen* per bowl ever since, but Yin's Bowls of Tea Trading Company is now a big business, with 18 outlets and 900 employees in 1989.

The secret of his success is in recreating the ambience of the old Beijing teahouses. The main location is in a shiny new shopping center that also houses Kentucky Fried Chicken. It looks anything but traditional from the outside, but once you enter you feel you have stepped back in time. In the center of the teahouse there is a stage where opera and folk singers, as well as story-tellers and musicians perform every night. Even in the daytime, the place has a charming and relaxing atmosphere. It was a pleasure to sip tea there and enjoy snacks of homemade pastries, dried fruits and nuts. We felt we had really had a glance at Old Beijing.

How to get there:

3 Qianmenxi Dajie, Xuanwu District.

宣武区前门西大街3号。

The Church of the Immaculate Conception

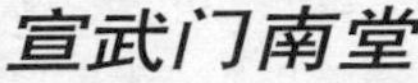

This is the most illustrious Catholic cathedral in Beijing, the original having been erected in 1650 by Adam Schall on the site of the Portuguese Mission. It was destroyed by fire and rebuilt in the time of Emperor Qianlong (1736-1796). It was closed in 1827 at the order of Emperor Daoguang, but was saved from confiscation by the Portuguese bishop of Beijing, who signed the property over to the Russian Orthodox mission.

In 1860 the building was handed back to Monsignor Joseph-Martial Mouly by the commander of the French invasion force. The French influence survives in a statute of Our Lady of Lourdes in a grotto in the grounds. The cathedral was again destroyed by fire in the early days of the Boxer Movement in 1900, and hundreds of Chinese Catholics perished in the flames or were massacred. The present building dates from 1904. Popularly known as the South Church, it functioned throughout the "cultural revolution" and survived unscathed.

A young nun showed us around in 1993. She told us that about 400 converts are baptised there every year. There are two training courses a year for nuns, with about 50 attending each course. The congregation at Sunday masses is around 2,000.

On the wall behind the pulpit is an oil painting of the Virgin Mary; to the left is a portrait of St. Joseph, and to the right one of the Sacred Heart of Jesus. Other paintings represent scenes from the life of Christ.

We visited the cathedral again in 1995. Fr. Laurence Shiyu Kun told us that they receive 200-300 visitors a day. There is an English mass at 10 a.m. every Sunday.

How to get there:

141 Qianmenxi Dajie, Xuanwu District.

宣武区前门西大街 141 号。

The Ox Street Mosque

牛街清真寺

From the outside, the mosque could be mistaken for a Chinese Taoist or Buddhist temple, until you notice that it is laid out on an east-west axis. This is because Moslems face Mecca when praying, and from China Mecca lies to the west. Nearly all Chinese places of worship, as well as the palaces of the Forbidden City, face south, as evil influences were supposed to originate in the north, and auspicious buildings had to turn their back on that direction.

The Ox Street Mosque is the oldest in Beijing, having been founded about 1,000 years ago. In the course of several reconstructions, Chinese architectural features have supplanted the original Islamic influences.

Inside the front gate is the Moon Watching Tower. This is where the imam observes the waxing and waning of the moon in order to decide when the fasting month of Ramadan begins and ends. In front of the tower is a memorial archway and a screen wall covered with carved murals. Beyond is the main prayer hall.

To the rear of the main prayer hall is a group of smaller halls, some of which are used as classrooms, and stele pavilions. There is also a bathhouse. The wall decorations consist of Arabic letters and geometrical patterns. There is an inscription in Arabic and Chinese dating from 1496, but over the centuries it has become illegible. In the center of this section there is a minaret from which the muezzin calls the faithful to prayer five times a day, beginning at

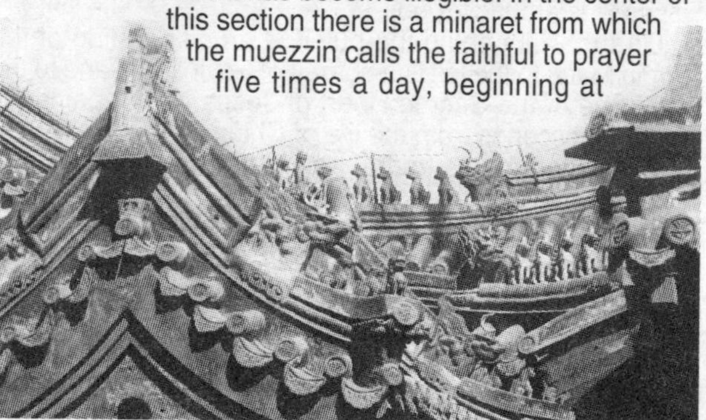

dawn.

In the grounds are the tombs of two travelers, one from Iran and the other from Uzbekistan.

Islam was probably introduced to China in the Tang Dynasty, and now four percent of China's population is Muslim. Beijing has some 210,000 Muslims. Relations between Muslims and non-Muslims have been strained in the past. It is said that a Chinese butcher would open a pork shop opposite the shop of a Muslim butcher. In order to frighten the sheep that were brought to the Muslim shop, he would paint a huge tiger in front of his own shop. The Muslim butcher would then hang up a large mirror so that the reflection of the tiger would devour the pigs in the pork shop.

During the "cultural revolution," when religious buildings were under attack, the personal intervention of the late Premier Zhou Enlai saved the Ox Street Mosque from destruction.

How to get there:

Niujie Street, Xuanwu District.

宣武区牛街。

The Temple of the Law

法源寺

This temple, the Fayuansi, located outside the Xuanwu city gate, in the southwest part of Beijing, is one of the oldest temples in the capital. It was first built during the Tang Dynasty, and named the Temple in Memory of the Loyal. It was rebuilt in the reign of Ming Emperor Zhengtong (1436-1449), and renamed the Temple of Exalted Happiness. The present name dates from 1734.

It houses some fine old relics: Bronze sculptures of the Four Heavenly Kings and lions date from the Ming Dynasty, as do rare gilded figures of three Buddhas, which stand on a "10,000 Buddhas" bronze platform. A huge stone urn in the shape of an alms bowl stands on a double support. In addition, there are old stelae, stone carvings and stone pillars.

The Scripture Library is located in the tranquil backyard of the temple. It can be entered only through the Dabei Hall. In the library there is a reclining Buddha, 7.4 meters long, made of wood.

The Fayuansi was once famous for its lilac gardens, being known as the "temple of fragrant snow." In the courtyard, there are pines dating from the Tang Dynasty, and cypresses which were planted in the Song Dynasty stand before the drum and bell towers. A ginkgo also said to be several hundred years old is growing next to the sutra tower.

How to get there:

7 Fayuansi Qianjie, Xuanwu District.

宣武区法源寺前街7号。

The Temple of Heavenly Peace

天宁寺

This is the oldest extant building in Beijing, dating from the Liao Dynasty (907-1125). It is not accessible, but can be observed from a distance.

In the form of an octagonal pagoda, the temple rests on a large square platform, and is composed of three sections–the base, the body and the 13-story tower. The edifice is 578 meters tall and made entirely of stone blocks. The base has a single band of arched niches carved in relief. Above this, the perimeter of the platform is decorated with brackets and balusters. These are surmounted by three rows of carved lotus petals. The lower part of the pagoda is decorated with large arched openings and relief carvings. Bells hanging from each story tinkle in the wind. The summit of the pagoda is decorated with a pearl-shaped symbol of the Buddhist faith.

How to get there:

North of Tianningsi Overpass, Xuanwu District.

宣武区天宁寺桥北。

The Altar of Grain

先农坛

This site, to the west of the Temple of Heaven, was where emperors prayed for good harvests every year. The altar and adjoining ceremonial buildings were built in 1420.

We visited it in 1989, and found that it had become a run-down area of factories, schools and a sports stadium. Since then, there have been efforts at restoration.

The decline began in the 1920s, when it was made into a martyrs' memorial park. After 1949, three factories, two middle schools, a pharmaceuticals research institute and a sports stadium were located there. Most of the ancient trees which once stood here have vanished, the sole survivor being a cypress protected by a fence. A few of the original structures have survived, but they are badly damaged. The marble platform from which the emperor surveyed his private field, which he symbolically tilled as part of the annual ritual, is still there, but the field has become a basketball court. The ceremonial kitchen, slaughterhouse and grain store have all been displaced by factories.

The Jufudian, the hall where the emperor changed into ceremonial attire, is now a school library. The Taisuidian, a complex of build-ings containing the altar of the God of the Harvest, was being restored when we were there, with glazed tiles and a plaque bearing the calligraphy of Emperor Qianlong.

How to get there:

Yongdingmen Dajie, Xuanwu District.

宣武区永定门大街。

Taoranting Park

陶然亭公园

This park in the southwest part of Beijing derives its name from the Joyous Pavilion that once stood in the grounds of the now-vanished Temple of Mercy. Before that, it had been the site of the brick kilns for the construction of the new capital when the Ming Dynasty replaced that of the Yuan.

The park is heavily forested, with carefully laid-out lakes and islets, and a number of pagodas in various styles. It is the place to go if you want to hear amateur Peking Opera fans practicing. They are all over the park, some singing alone and others singing with instrumental accompaniment.

How to get there:

19 Taiping Street, Xuanwu District.

宣武区太平街19号。

The Xu Beihong School

徐悲鸿中学

Our group visited the school set up by Xu Beihong's widow and son in 1995 in the painter's memory. We went at the invitation of my friend Ye Xue, who teaches there.

The Xu Beihong Middle School is a large, well-lighted building with a charming atrium. There are over 400 pupils, of whom 50 are boarders.

As befits the legacy of one of modern China's greatest painters, art is a strong subject at the school, which has fully-equipped studios. We were impressed by the quality of the children's traditional Chinese paintings, oils and pencil drawings, as well as their skill in tie-dyeing, pottery and weaving.

The staff and students gave us a warm welcome, and they even served us a very tasty lunch.

How to get there:

Jia 10 Youneixi Dajie, Xuanwu District.

宣武区右内西大街甲10号。

The Grand View Garden

大观园

This is a reproduction of the garden which provides the setting for much of the intrigue in the Qing Dynasty classical novel *A Dream of Red Mansions*. Constructed in 1986, it was used for making the movie and TV series versions of the novel.

Set out as a park, the garden is an authentic reflection of the grounds of an aristocratic mansion in old China. There are over 40 structures and scenic spots, including the Bamboo Garden, the Hall of Spring, and Red Happiness Lodge, which was the living quarters of the hero Jia Baoyu.

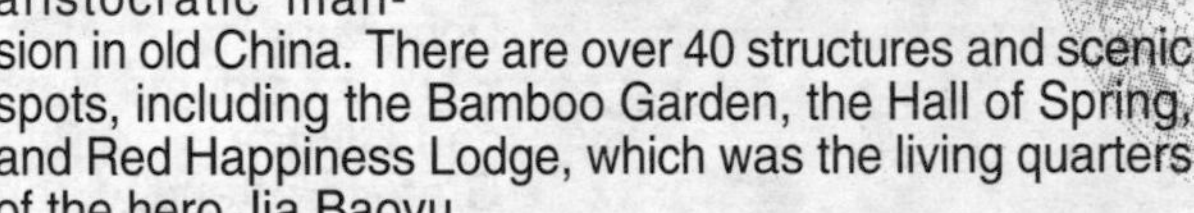

A visit to the Grand View Garden is a good introduction to this monumental novel, and should inspire those who have not already done so to become acquainted with its dozens of unforgettable characters and vivid pictures of a bygone age. On display are the costumes worn by the actors in the TV and movie scenes, as well as pictures of various episodes.

How to get there:

12 Nancaiyuan Street, Xuanwu District.

宣武区南菜园街 12 号。

The Chongwenmen Church

崇文门堂

This is the largest Protestant church in Beijing, with two services every Sunday, as well as one in the Korean language. The number of worshippers is in excess of 2000 at every service, and in the warm weather, people stand in the courtyard and watch the proceedings on closed-circuit TV. The chapel part of the auditorium also has TV monitors, as the worshippers are not able to see the pulpit. In-stantaneous translation into English is provided via cordless head-phones.

The church was formerly the Methodist Mission in Beijing, and was re-opened in 1981. Protestant believers had been holding services in the YMCA building on Dongdan.

US presidents Bush and Clinton, and Billy Graham attended services in the Chongwenmen church on their visits to Beijing.

There used to be a Methodist school next to the church, with a sign reading "The Mary Gamewell Porter School," but it has been replaced by an office building.

How to get there:

Ding 2 Hougou Hutong Chongwenmennei, Chongwen District.

崇文区崇文门内后沟胡同丁2号。

The Old Beijing City Wall

老北京城墙遗址

Most of the Beijing City Wall was demolished in the early 1960s, and the moat was filled in to make way for the Second Ring Road and the subway system. But remnants of the wall dating from the Ming Dynasty can still be found in the southwest corner of the old city, and even a few segments of the Jin and Yuan dynasty walls.

In 1996, there was a drive to collect bricks from the wall which people had taken away when it was torn down, to be used for renovating parts of the old wall. These were special bricks, weighing 20 kg each. They were manufactured in Shandong Province or in Tianjin, and brought to Beijing along the Grand Canal as ballast for rice barges.

Our group's explorations in 1989 found that the Dongbianmen Gate is a good place to glimpse the original architecture of the wall. The large pillars and beams, and the ladders that connect the stories of the gate tower are intact. The Ming wall was built using two rows of rock slabs as the base. Many of the exposed bricks at Dongbianmen bear inscriptions; one was dated to the spring of a certain year during the reign of Emperor Jiaqing, and mentioned the name of the construction foreman of that section.

Dongbianmen was called the "Fox Tower," as it was said to be haunted by a fox spirit, an evil apparition, according to Chinese mythology. Doors were left open for his ghostly comings and goings. The gate was shelled by the Russians during the Boxer Movement, but it has since been repaired, and hosts furniture and art exhibitions from time to time.

How to get there:

Dongbianmen Gate, Chongwenmendong Dajie, Chongwen District.

崇文区崇文门东大街东便门。

The Temple of Heaven or Tiantan Park

天坛公园

Located in southeastern Beijing, the Temple of Heaven occupies 273 hectares, more than twice the area of the Imperial Palace. It was begun during the reign of Emperor Yongle (1403-1425) of the Ming Dynasty, and took 14 years to complete. The Qing Dynasty emperors Qianlong and Jiaqing had the temple expanded. It was the site of imperial sacrifices to Heaven during the Ming and Qing periods, a total of over 500 years.

The three main structures are circular, corresponding to the supposed shape of Heaven. They have deep-blue glazed tile roofs and a platform each constructed of slabs of white marble. Each of the three platforms consists of three tiers, making a total of nine, a mystic number said to be the epitome of *yang*, or the positive principle of the Universe and signifying Heaven.

The Temple of Heaven originally had only one main gate, which faced west, but when it was made a public park in 1949 entrances were opened on the northern, southern and eastern sides as well. The Bridge of Cinnabar Steps (Danbiqiao), which is really a walkway, connects the main structures of the temple–The Hall of Prayer for a Good Harvest (Qiniandian) to the north, and the Hall of the Imperial Heavenly Vault (Huangqiongyu) and the Altar of Heaven (Huanqiu) to the south.

The wall which encloses the southern end of the temple grounds is square, but the northern end is semi-circular, based on the ancient notion that the Earth is square and Heaven round. Old cypress trees surround the buildings, giving them a venerable atmosphere.

The Altar of Heaven consists of three tiers of green and white marble, with a white marble balustrade around each tier. The surface of the platform, the stairs and the railings are all made of stone slabs, again in multiples of nine. The top platform is 33.3 meters in diameter. The circular stone in the center was considered the most sacred spot in the Chinese empire. Around it, the first ring of stones consists of nine slabs, the second ring of 18, the third of 27, and so forth until the ninth and outermost row consists of 81 stones. The central and lower levels are also made up of nine concentric rings of stones, again laid out in multiples of nine.

An unusual aspect of the Temple of Heaven is acoustic phenomena. If you stand in the center of the altar and speak softly, you can hear the echo of your own voice, but the people near you can't. This is because the sound bounces off the surrounding balustrade and returns directly to the center of the circle. Nearby Echo Wall offers something similar. This is a circular wall of polished bricks enclosing the Imperial Vault of Heaven, which is a three-tiered circular marble altar with a gilded tapering roof that looks like a spread umbrella. Also within the wall are the East Hall and the West Hall. If you stand whispering at one end of Echo Wall, another person standing 60 meters away at the other end, with the two halls in between, can hear distinctly what is being said. Then if you stand on the first flagstone at the bottom of the staircase which leads to the southern door of the Hall of the Imperial Heavenly Vault and clap or shout, a single echo is heard; standing on the second stone, a double echo is heard; and on the third stone, a triple echo.

The genius of traditional Chinese architecture can be seen in the construction of the main hall. Instead of iron nails, cement or reinforcing rods, the whole structure is supported by wooden mortise and tenon joints and wooden brackets on huge supporting pillars. There are altogether 28 pillars, of red-lacquered *nanmu* (a hardwood) symbolizing the 28 constellations. The four central pillars are the thickest and are painted with gilded coiling dragons, symbolizing the four seasons. The twelve pillars around them symbolize the 12 months of the lunar calendar, while beyond them is an outer circle of 12, symbolizing the 12 two-hour periods into which the day and night were divided in ancient China. Altogether, the 24 pillars represent the 24 solar periods of the traditional Chinese calendar.

Inside the hall, the ceiling is carved in a design of dragons and phoenixes. The floor is paved with flagstones, in the center of which is a slab of marble with natural veining resembling a dragon and phoenix design. The hall retains its original furnishings of a long table, a throne and screens.

In front of the hall are an incense burner decorated with the eight trigrams which were used in divination and were thought to hold the secrets of the universe, and a bronze tripod. These objects are several hundred years old.

How to get there:

North of Tianqiao Dajie, Chongwen District.

崇文区天桥大街北。

Yuyuantan Park

玉渊潭公园

This park is located in Haidian District, and is a favorite venue for shows and exhibitions of all descriptions. In 1994, we went there to see a lantern show, the theme of which was the Three Gorges Dam project on the upper reaches of the Yangtze River. In the summer of the following year, we visited an Acrobatic Cultural Village which had been set up in the park.

The performers were all from the same village in Hebei Province. They are renowned for their acrobatic skills, which have been handed down from generation to generation. There was a woman lying on her back and juggling her nine-year-old daughter on the soles of her feet. Other feats of strength, skill and magic included one in which a man played a merry tune on the *suona*, a traditional Chinese woodwind instrument, while a 100-kg millstone pressed down on his chest. Not far away, a young girl juggled a 150-kg water vat with her feet, with a man squatting inside. There were fire eaters and a man who specialized in threading thin sticks up his nose and out through his eyes.

How to get there:

Sanlihe Road, Haidian District.

海淀区三里河路。

The Five-Pagoda Temple

真觉寺

This is also known as the Zhenjuesi, Great Awakening Temple. The main temple building, known as the Diamond Throne, and the five pagodas show strong Indian influence. Construction started in the early years of the Ming Dynasty Emperor Yongle (1403-1413) and was completed in the reign of Emperor Chenghua (1473). The design was suggested to Yongle by a visiting Indian monk named Pancha Charma, who presented the emperor with five golden statues of Buddha.

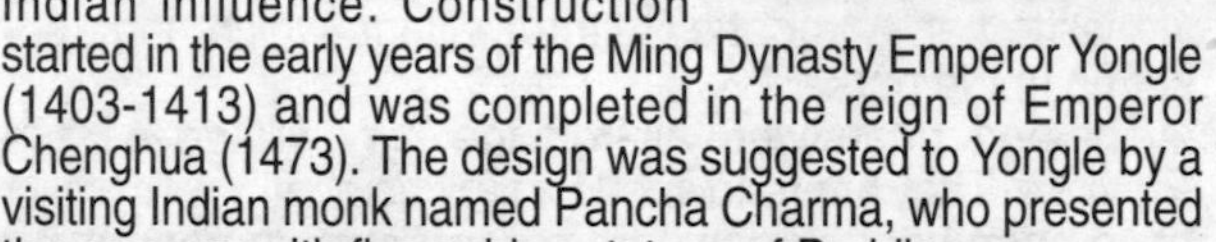

The five pagodas are built on a single platform, known as the Diamond Throne, in imitation of the Gaya Temple in the state of Bihar in India, where Buddha is said to have gained enlightenment. The carvings around the base are of elephants, lions, phoenixes, the wheel of life surrounded by flames and endless knots. Carved on the base of the middle pagoda is a life-size pair of feet, representing the feet of Sakyamuni on his deathbed.

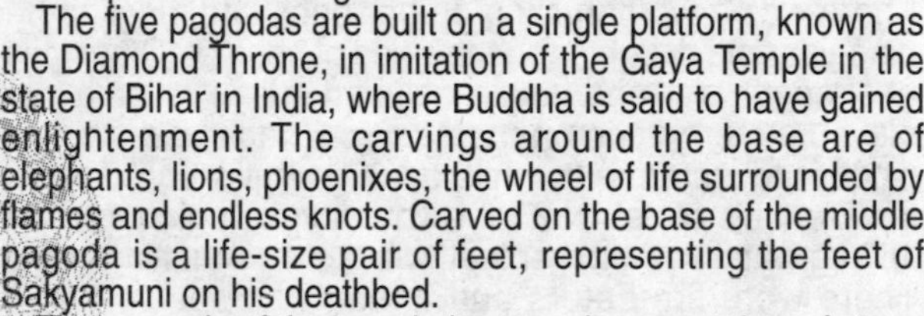

The grounds of the temple house a large number of stone carvings and steles which have been unearthed or moved from their original sites in the course of urban construction. The more interesting pieces were an altar for making offerings to ancestors, and ancient stone tomb chamber, a stone turtle bearing a stele erected to honor a person still living at the time, dated 1749. There is a section for epitaphs, some dating as far back as the Han Dynasty. These carved stones often bear depictions of the animals of the Chinese zodiac, including animal heads and human bodies.

On our second visit to the temple, in 1997, we noticed that some tombstones of foreigners had been included, with Christian symbols and inscriptions in English, Latin and Chinese. Most dated from the 19th century, but one was as early as 1759.

How to get there:

Baishiqiao Road, Haidian District.

海淀区白石桥路。

Purple Bamboo Park

紫竹院公园

This park is one of Beijing's largest. It is situated at the southern end of White Marble Bridge Road, with its eastern gate directly opposite the Capital Gymnasium. It has three connecting lakes, which occupy 11 of the park's 14 hectares. Earth dredged from the lakes was piled up to form several small hills on the eastern shores, to match natural hills on the western shores. Five bridges connect the lakes, islets and hills.

The area was originally a reservoir supplying Beijing, and was converted into rice paddies during the first half of the 20th century. In the 1950s it was made into a park, with lush bamboo groves, shady trees and open-air pavilions. In 1981, a two-story waterside complex was opened. This consists of the Purple Bamboo Pavilion, the Gallery for Watching the Moon, a winding walkway that leads out over the water and a square pavilion. Each structure is independent, but from a distance they seem to blend into one.

The lakes are famous for their gorgeous lotus flowers, and boat rides are popular in summer, as is skating in winter.

How to get there:

45 Baishiqiao Road, Haidian District.

海淀区白石桥路 45 号。

The Central Dance Academy

北京舞蹈学院

The Academy is divided into two parts: the middle, junior and senior high school streams, with 400 students (most often referred to as the Beijing Dance Institute), and the college, which can accommodate 300 students.

In 1993, we were given a tour of the Academy by Zhao Guowei, a teacher there. After lunch, she took us to her apartment, where her daughter-in-law treated us to a recital on the *pipa*, or Chinese mandolin.

Several of China's large cities have dance academies at the middle school level, but this is the only one with a tertiary-level institution with places reserved for the most outstanding pupils. It offers ballet, classical Chinese dance and Chinese folk dance. Built in 1954, the Academy has 42 classrooms with high ceilings and large windows. There is a distinctly Soviet flavor about the architecture.

We watched a girls' ballet class, a "pas-de-deux" class and a classical Chinese dance class. The students were so focussed that they seemed hardly to be aware of our presence.

The top graduates go on to take the college-level courses, and then join China's leading dance troupes or become dance teachers.

We were fortunate enough to have a British ballet teacher as one of our group on this occasion. She noted that the students were extremely pliant, with excellent backs and very high leg extensions.

As a follow-up to the visit, we were invited to see a performance of "Fish Beauty" by students of the Academy.

How to get there:

19 Minzuxueyuan (Institute for Nationalities) Nanlu, Haidian District.

海淀区民族学院南路 19 号。

The Wanshou (Long Life) Temple

万寿寺

This temple is situated on the Changhe River, in the western part of the city. It was built in 1578 at the order of Empress Dowager Li, the mother of Emperor Wanli of the Ming Dynasty. On his mother's birthdays in 1751 and 1761, Qing Dynasty Emperor Qianlong had it repaired and expanded.

It became an imperial temple when gardens and a temporary palace, where the imperial family stopped on their way to the Summer Palace, were added. The temple is now the Beijing Art Museum. Our group has visited it several times. One visit was particularly memorable, because there were folk artists making exquisite dolls and dressing them in traditional court costumes. Some of them, we were told, were to be given to visiting heads of state.

How to get there:

In Suzhoujie, Haidian District.

海淀区苏州街。

The Big Bell Temple

大钟寺

This temple dates from 1733, when it was called the Temple of Righteous Awakening. After a giant bell was transferred here from the Temple of Longevity in 1743, the name was changed to Big Bell Temple (Dazhongsi).

There are three main buildings. In front of the first one stands an unusual tree–a cypress with an elm branch grafted onto its trunk. The famous bell hangs in a tower in the rear of the compound. The tower is 16.7 m high, with a square base, a circular upper structure and windows on all four sides.

The bronze bell was cast in the Yongle period (1403-1424) of the Ming Dynasty by master craftsman Yao Guangxiao. It is 6.87 m high, 3.3 m in diameter, 0.22 m thick and weighs 46.5 tons. It is said that, when struck, the bell can be heard 50 km away. Carved on the surface of the bell, both inside and outside, is the full text of the Huayan Sutra, all 80 chapters and comprising 220,000 characters. On account of this, the bell is sometimes called the "Huayan Bell."

We visited the Big Bell Temple in 1994, on the occasion of an international bell festival. There were bells old and new, big and tiny on display, and performances of bell ringing, singing and dancing were held.

How to get there:

Jia 31 Beisanhuan Xilu, Haidian District.

海淀区北三环西路甲 31 号。

Siheyuan, or Courtyard Houses

四合院

Courtyard houses are traditional Beijing dwellings, and the style dates from the Yuan Dynasty. With the modernization of the city, however, they are fast disappearing, along with the narrow alleys, or *hutongs*, which snake between them.

In May 1996, we learned about the history and structure of these "*siheyuan*" from Prof. Wang Qiming of the Beijing College of Architecture. She first started to study them in 1958. At that time, the stretch of Chang'an Avenue between Dongdan and Xidan was actually two cramped streets with courtyard houses in between. As Chang'an is the city's main thoroughfare, the houses were slated for demolition, and Prof. Wang was given the task of surveying and recording these relics of old Beijing.

One of the main features of these constructions is that they have no weight-bearing walls; pillars and beams sustain all the weight of the roof. So there is a saying that "the walls may fall down, but the roof will not fall in."

As the name "*siheyuan*" implies, the layout of these houses comprises a central courtyard, with rooms or detached buildings on all four sides. Commonly, the main entrance is an open gateway, guarded just inside by a "spirit screen." This is a wall preventing passers-by peering into the courtyard, although folklore has it that it stops evil spirits, which apparently can only travel in straight lines, penetrating the household. The quarters of the master of the house face the courtyard and the south, an auspicious direction. It often has annexes–known as "ear houses," on either side. Sometimes there are two, or even three, courtyards, separated from each other by "hanging flower" gates. In the latter case, there is another set of buildings behind the main one.

We later visited some courtyard houses, albeit rather grand ones, in Haidian District, which is on the route to Summer Palace. The first one is known as Jiya Tong, meaning "chicken and duck seller," because that was where the merchant who supplied chickens, ducks and eggs to

the imperial palace lived. The story goes that his fortunes declined and he had to sell the house after Qing Emperor Qianlong disguised himself as a commoner and found out that the "chicken and duck seller" had been cheating him. The house was bought by a senior official named Wang Wenxiao, who decorated it lavishly and installed a large covered stage for opera performances. The house was confiscated after the 1911 revolution, and now houses the No. 44 Primary School.

Next we were shown around a dwelling formerly occupied by Empress Dowager Cixi's favorite eunuch, and now partly occupied by the Haidian Health Bureau. This is probably the best-preserved *siheyuan* in Beijing. The main buildings have gilt-embossed doors and carved fretwork borders around the glass panes in the doors and windows. We saw original stone work called "tiger skin walls," and corridors which had formerly been decorated with raised scenes from *A Dream of Red Mansions*. The scenes were plastered over during the "cultural revolution."

The third courtyard house we visited was Li Wang's Palace, much of which is now the August First Middle School. There are plans to move the school to new premises and restore the mansion.

The house was built by a prince during the reign of Emperor Qianlong. It is elaborate and spacious, and it has been suggested that it was the model for the Grand View Garden of the classical novel *A Dream of Red Mansions*. It has the Main Hall, East Hall and Reverse Hall (facing the wrong way). The main hall was for audiences and discussions of affairs of state; opposite was a place for drinking tea and watching artistic performances. The grounds boast a terrace, a rockery and a pond with a pavilion accessible by a stepping-stone bridge.

The Sackler Museum

北大赛克勒考古与艺术博物馆

Located just inside the western entrance to Beijing University (Beida), the Sackler Museum was opened in 1994.

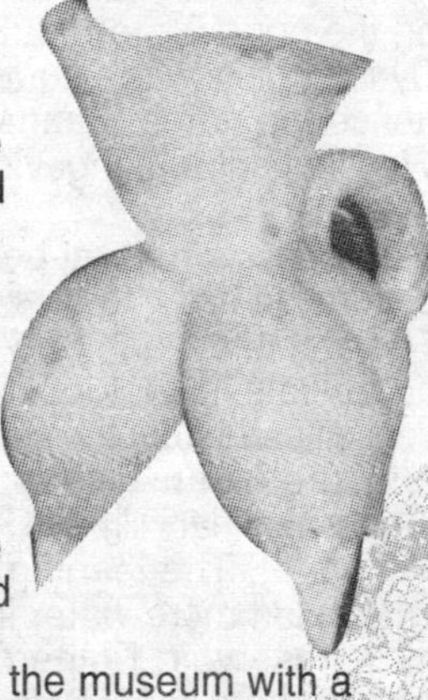

The objects on display include animal fossils, stone tools, and ceramic and bronze wares. They are arranged in 14 galleries, grouping relics from the Paleolithic period right up to the Ming Dynasty. They are also arranged according to context, such as tomb excavations and geographical location. The labeling is in both Chinese and English.

We combined our visit to the museum with a stroll around the nearby No Name Lake, the pagoda and the grave of Edgar Snow, author of the epoch-making *Red Star Over China*.

How to get there:

In Beijing University, Haidian District.

海淀区北京大学校内。

The Summer Palace

颐和园

The Yiheyuan, or Palace of Nurtured Harmony, is located on the northwestern outskirts of Beijing. From the Yuan Dynasty on, it was a summer retreat for the imperial family, hence the name Summer Palace. Its main features are Wanshoushan (Longevity Hill) and Kunminghu (Kunming Lake).

The park's natural beauty is set off by a host of very decorative halls, towers, galleries, pavilions and bridges. The architects adapted the buildings to blend in with or accentuate the natural surroundings in an ingenious way, very different from the courtyard style of the Forbidden City.

In the Yuan Dynasty, Wanshoushan was called Wengshan (Jar Hill) and Kunminghu was Wengshanpo (Jar Hill pond). The leading engineer-official Guo Shoujing channeled more water in to expand the pond to make a large reservoir. Emperor Qianlong began construction projects here in 1750, to celebrate the 60th birthday of his mother the following year. The renovation work went on for 15 years. In 1860, the Anglo-French invasion forces plundered and destroyed much of the Summer Palace, along with other imperial parks. The park was restored, beginning in 1885, using funds earmarked for the setting up of a naval academy. A poignant reminder of the origin of the funds is a huge marble replica of a boat "moored" by the shore of Kunming Lake. In 1889, the Empress Dowager Cixi retired to the Yiheyuan, from which she fled in 1900, when the Allied forces invaded Beijing. The park was damaged once again. In 1914, the park was opened to the public for an admission fee by the imperial family, and when the last emperor, Puyi, fled from Beijing in 1924, it became a public park.

The Long Corridor is the longest in the history of China's landscape gardening. 728 meters long, it was first built in 1750. The present structure dates from the reign of Emperor Guangxu (1875-1908). It bears 14,000 colorful paintings, with themes from Chinese history, mythology and tradition. In the Palace of Parting Clouds, is a unique oil portrait of Empress Dowager Cixi done by Katherine A. Carl, an American who also wrote a book about Cixi. Although Cixi was 69 years old when the portrait was painted, it represents her as a woman of about 30. The Garden of Harmonious Virtue contains the stage where the imperial family watched operas. In one of the halls of the Garden is a collection of antique vehicles, including an early-model motor car given to Cixi by one of the world's first auto makers.

The Summer Palace is a popular spot for Beijingers all the year round, with boating on Kunming Lake in summer and ice skating in winter.

How to get there:

In Haidian District, 15 km from downtown Beijing.

北京海淀区，距市区约 15 公里。

Yuanmingyuan

圆明园

This imperial garden is not far from the Summer Palace. Construction started in about 1700, and went on for about 150 years. The main buildings were in classical European style, and the whole was supposed to be a sort of "Versailles of the East." The whole of the Yuanmingyuan was plundered and razed to the ground by the Anglo-French invasion forces in 1860.

On our first visit, we found only ruins, but on every subsequent visit we perceived that more and more restoration work was being done. A maze and a small pavilion at its center have been fully restored. There are now more than 10,000 trees in the park, which covers an area of more than 5,200 *mu* (over 800 acres), with winding paths and landscaped scenery, making the Yuanmingyuan a favorite spot for picnics.

Special exhibitions are held here from time to time, including the annual Chrysanthemum Festival in the fall.

How to get there:

28 Qinghuaxi Road, Haidian District.

海淀区清华西路28号。

The Azure Cloud Temple

碧云寺

The Biyunsi, or Azure Cloud Temple, is located on the eastern slopes of the Fragrant Hills (Xiangshan), in the western suburbs of Beijing. It was first built in the early 14th century as the private residence of a Yuan Dynasty court official. It was converted into a Buddhist temple in 1366, and expanded in the early 16th century and again in 1748, during the reign of Qing Dynasty Emperor Qianlong. The latter expansion saw the erection of the Hall of the Immortals in the southern courtyard and the Diamond Throne Pagoda in the rear. The present temple is the result of renovation in 1954.

The Diamond Throne Pagoda is where the body of Sun Yat-sen, the founder of modern China, lay in state, following his death in 1925, until it was removed to the Sun Yat-sen Mausoleum in Nanjing in 1929. Some of his clothing and personal effects are still in the pagoda. One of the Biyunsi's four main halls is now the Sun Yat-sen Memorial Hall, and contains a bust of Sun and a bronze-and-glass coffin. The coffin was a gift from the Soviet Union, but as it arrived two weeks after Sun's remains had been entombed it was never used.

The Hall of the Immortals (Luohantang), designed in the shape of a Greek cross, houses 500 gilded wooden images of Buddhist saints and seven Buddha statues. These are examples of Qing Dynasty wood carving, and each has its own individual personality and expression. A curiosity is an image of a monk known as Master Jigong squatting on a rafter. Legend has it that he arrived late for prayers one day, could not find a seat, and because of his junior rank had to climb onto the rafter.

How to get there:

Located in the Fragrant Hills Park in Haidian District.

海淀区香山公园内。

Prince Yixuan's Tomb

七王坟

Prince Yixuan was the father of Qing Dynasty Emperor Guangxu. He early incurred the enmity of his sister-in-law, the powerful Empress Dowager Cixi, and decided to extricate himself from court intrigues. At the age of 33, he started to look for a good spot to spend the rest of eternity, and was assisted in his quest by Cixi, who allocated 50,000 ounces of silver from the national treasury to build his tomb.

Just before Prince Yixuan's death, in 1890, Cixi had already asserted her authority over her nephew Emperor Guangxu, to the extent of forbidding him to visit his father on his deathbed. Seven years later, she ordered the uprooting of a gingko tree from the vicinity of the prince's tomb, claiming that it represented continued rebellion against her rule.

The tomb is located in the sleepy village of Qiwangfen (Prince's Village), in the Western Hills. The graveyard is approached by a staircase to a pavilion, in which there is a huge stone turtle bearing a stele that tells the history of the graveyard. The pavilion was completely exposed to the elements in 1993, when we first visited it, but has been repaired since, as have the rest of the grounds.

A marble bridge crosses a riverbed to a yard containing two bare rooms, which were once the quarters of the tomb keepers. Behind, lie the graves of the prince and his consort, and his three concubines. The area is thick with pine trees.

How to get there:

In Beianhe Village, Haidian District.

海淀区北安河乡。

The Dajue Temple

大觉寺

This temple is located in a remote spot northwest of Beijing, on the eastern side of Mount Yangtai, a peak that looks like a crouching lion. It was originally built in the Liao Dynasty, and named the Clear Spring Temple after the stream that ran through the temple grounds. It was given its present name when it was rebuilt in 1428. An unusual feature of the temple is that it faces east, instead of south.

The Dajue Temple was favored by the imperial court, and Emperor Qianlong and Empress Dowager Cixi wrote inscriptions for it. In the Mahavira Hall, the main hall of the temple, there is a seated statue of Sakyamuni surrounded by 20 statues called *zuntian*, a sort of Boddhisatva, each with a different gesture and facial expression. There is a celebrated statue of Guanyin, the Goddess of Mercy, in another hall.

In the grounds there is a giant gingko tree, said to be 1, 000 years old, a pool formed of giant white stone slabs, and ancient magnolia trees. On the top of the temple is a Liao Dynasty pagoda embraced by a cypress and a pine.

How to get there:

In Beianhe Village, Haidian District.

海淀区北安河乡。

The Military Drill Ground

团城演武厅

This elliptical area is located at the southern foot of the Fragrant Hills. It was constructed in 1749, in the 14th year of the reign of Emperor Qianlong. It is 50.2 meters from east to west, and 40 meters from north to south. The north and south gates carry inscriptions in Qianlong's calligraphy.

There is a platform at one end with the throne on which the emperor sat to review the troops practicing their various drills in the arena, which is paved with black bricks. The western tower, with an arched gate, represented a city, and around it the soldiers would demonstrate their siege warfare skills.

There is a small museum displaying ancient weapons and reproductions of the uniforms of the Eight Banner armies of the Qing Dynasty. These were crack Manchu units organized under eight flags of different colors. There is a picture of a scene of soldiers of that time drilling and a portrait of Emperor Qianlong in martial attire.

How to get there:

1 Hongqi Village Xiangshannanlu, Haidian District.

海淀区香山南路红旗村1号。

The Dragon Spring Temple
龙泉寺

Dating from the Liao Dynasty (904-1125), the Dragon Spring Temple (Longquansi) suffered the indignity of being turned into a chicken farm until it was rescued by the local villagers in 1996 and restored, being given a *kaiguang*, or opening blessing, by a Buddhist priest. Some huge gingko trees in the grounds are said to date back to the temple's founding.

The first hall houses a highly gilded smiling Buddha. Three more Buddha images are located in the second hall. The central one is Amitabha, and he is flanked by the Buddha of Medicine, who aids believers in this life, and the Buddha of Transition, who helps believers to make a peaceful crossing to the next life. The temple's statues were made using the traditional method of sculpting clay around a wooden framework, although some untraditional nails were also used.

Longquansi is located on Mount Fenghuangling, at a point where the north-south and east-west hills protecting Beijing meet. These hills are covered in cedar trees, and there are log cabins provided by the temple for overnight stays.

How to get there:

On Mount Fenghuangling in the Western Mountains Farm, Haidian District.
海淀区西山农场境内凤凰岭自然风景区。

The Western Waterway

京西水道

In 1993, our group went by bus and on foot to explore the old western waterway of the capital. This system was also the work of Guo Shoujing, and connected the Grand Canal with the Eastern Waterway, and later with Kunming Lake in the Summer Palace to the northwest of Beijing. This northwest corner is high enough to allow water to flow naturally to the southern and eastern districts of the city.

In Yuan times, the capital extended further north than the present-day inner city, and the three back lakes were one stretch of water. The docks for receiving and distributing the tribute grain from the south were located at the northern end.

We first visited the Huitongci watergate, a 1988 reconstruction of the original, which was demolished in the 1960s along with the city wall. The watergate temple is now a museum dedicated to Guo Shoujing, containing diagrams and models of his ingenious designs for locks, weirs and overflow devices. Guo's astronomical discoveries are also on display. Beneath the approach bridge to the museum are carvings of two mythical water creatures, one to ensure the supply and the other to check it.

By the early Ming Dynasty, the eastern canal had silted up, and the lake had been divided into three by mudbanks. Water was then brought to the city from the western canal, entering at the spot where the Gaoliang Bridge

still stands. The water now goes underground at the bridge, so the c. 1320 lock is high and dry to the west.

The imperial family would leave the city by the Xizhimen Gate, and embark for the Summer Palace from just above this lock. In order to navigate "uphill," the Gaoliang lock, the lowest in the system, would be closed, while the other locks in the system were opened.

North along the canal, just east of the Five-Pagoda Temple (Wutasi), we came to the most famous drawbridge and lock on the canal, the Guangyuanqiao. The imperial family would disembark here, and wait at the nearby Wanshou Temple for the canal's upper reaches to fill.

Across the Third Ring Road, just north of the Shangri-La Hotel, lock foundations can be seen at the next bridge, and soon after that the old canal connects with the new one bringing water to Beijing from Miyun Reservoir.

How to get there:

In Haidian District.

海淀区。

Ritan Park

日坛公园

This park is near the Jianguomenwai diplomatic quarter, and is a favorite spot for morning exercises for both Chinese and non-Chinese. Martial arts enthusiasts and devotees of Taiji Quan, or Chinese slow-motion shadow boxing can be seen in all corners of the park very early in the morning, along with groups doing ballroom and folk dances.

As is the case with most Chinese parks, you will see older men exercising their birds. They do this by swinging their cages vigorously. This causes the birds to grip their perches firmly, which in turn strengthens their chest muscles and improves their ability to sing. The cages are then hung on tree branches, the covers removed and the birds allowed to sing to their hearts content. In the winter, the cages are always hung where they will get the maximum sunshine. I often see their owners digging in the flower beds for juicy worms and other insects to feed to their pets.

There are restaurants in the park that are very popular because of their excellent menus and reasonable prices. We often end our Tuesday outings with lunch at one of them, where, depending on the weather, we can dine "al-fresco."

How to get there:

Ritan Road, Jianguomenwai Dajie, Chaoyang District.

朝阳区建国门外大街日坛路。

Dong Yue Temple

东岳庙

On busy Chaoyang Road, filled with shop-ping malls and heavy traffic, visitors can find a haven from the noise and commotion of this huge city.

In March, 1999, the restored Dong Yue Taoist Temple was opened again, after being neglected for almost 100 years. It has large courtyards and is now more like a museum than a place of worship, though you will see many people praying, burning incense and leaving offerings here.

Construction of the Dong Yue Temple started in the 13th century, under the patronage of the Yuan Dynasty Emperor Wenzong. It was an important temple from the Ming Dynasty on, and continued to enjoy favor from the throne.

The temple fell into disrepair after the Qing Dynasty was toppled in 1911. Most of the thousands of images of Taoist gods in its shrines and linking courtyards were destroyed, especially by Red Guards during the "cultural revolution." However, the elaborate gold, blue and green ceilings, intricate eaves and the basic structure of the buildings are intact. The five-year restoration work has succeeded in recreating the original with slight adaptations.

How to get there:

In Chaoyangmenwai Dajie, Chaoyang District.

朝阳区朝阳门外大街。

The Yellow Temple

黄寺

This temple, also known as Huangsi, located in the Andingmen area of northern Beijing, also houses the Institute of Lamaism. It was built during the Ming Dynasty, but has been destroyed and rebuilt several times. The temple was where the Dalai Lama stayed on his visits to Beijing. It also received Mongolian dignitaries, who shared the Lamaist Buddhist faith.

In 1780, the Sixth Panchen Lama died at the temple, where he was staying during his visit on the occasion of the birthday of Emperor Qianlong. The emperor ordered a stone stupa to be built to hold the Panchen Lama's clothes. The stupa is decorated with scenes of the life of Buddha.

In 1991, we were shown around the temple by Mr Kinga of the Tibet Development Fund. He briefed us on the history of the temple and showed us the classrooms where young lamas are trained. Traditional Tibetan medicine is also taught here.

Finally, we were treated to Tibetan butter tea and delicacies.

Our visit seems to have been a unique occasion, because I have tried several times to take other groups there since, but have been firmly refused.

How to get there:

Huangsi Road, Andingmenwai, Chaoyang District.

朝阳区安定门外黄寺路。

The Yan Huang Art Museum

炎黄艺术馆

This museum, which opened in 1991, is situated in the Asian Games Village. It is Beijing's first modern privately run art gallery, although it does receive government subsidies.

The building exhibits many features of Tang and Song dynasty architecture, blending with contemporary approaches. It is roofed with aubergine purple tiles. The approach to the main entrance is lined with quaint rocks called "mushroom rocks," brought from the area of the Marco Polo Bridge, or Lugouqiao, outside Beijing.The front door was made by melting down old cannon shells. Inside, two bronze doors leading to the exhibition areas were donated by members of Taiwan's cultural and industrial circles.

The museum concentrates on collecting contemporary Chinese paintings, but there are also examples of old paintings and calligraphy. The nine exhibition halls can be opened up to form a large display area for exhibitions. They maximize the use of natural light and direct sunlight is prevented from falling on the pieces on display. The marble floors, display cases and lighting are all impressive.

On our visit in 1994, we saw collections of plum blossom paintings, ancient pottery and Buddhist sculptures.

How to get there:

9 Huizhong Road, Yayuncun (Asian Games Village), Chaoyang District.

朝阳区亚运村慧中路9号。

The Red Sandalwood Museum

紫檀博物馆

This museum, which opened on September 19, 1999, is in traditional Chinese architectural style, which harmonizes well with the furniture it displays. There are more than 1, 000 items of red sandalwood furniture and decorations in the 10 display rooms.

Red sandalwood is a very hard wood that emits a musty flower-like fragrance. In former times it was greatly prized for imperial court furniture. Some of the display rooms are designed like rooms in ancient mansions and are furnished in the style of the dynasty they represent.

A golden replica of the throne in the Imperial Palace is the first exhibit as one enters from the foyer. A smaller "golden lotus" throne is on display in another part of the Museum. Ming Dynasty furniture made of red sandalwood had simple lines and emphasized the natural beauty of the grain of the wood. Qing furniture is much more elaborate, with intricate patterns and fine craftsmanship; there is also more Western influence shown in the Qing period.

A particularly interesting piece is a replica of one of the corner towers of the Forbidden City. It is said that a Ming Dynasty emperor wanted a tower with nine beams and 18 columns. The architects were puzzled over how to design such a tower, but finally one got inspiration from the design of a bamboo cricket cage. The tower has nine beams, 18 columns and 72 ridges, adding up to 99, which is a very auspicious number, being the largest with two digits.

There is also a model of the Wanchun Pavilion (10,000 Springs) in the Imperial Garden in the Forbidden City as well as another pavilion from the Garden.

Chen Lihua is the curator of the museum, which she calls the "fulfilment of a dream." She has made many trips to Myanmar and India to buy red sandalwood, as well as other precious woods such as poplar, ebony, black sandalwood and hwang hua wood.

One room is arranged as a study in the Ming style, with desks, chairs, cabinets and bookshelves. Another is a replica of a traditional bedroom, with a moon gate entrance to the bed and a footstand with rollers for massaging the feet built into the bed. There is also a bridal chamber, complete with the double happiness symbol and satin bed curtains.

The wood, we were told, has special health benefits, and we were advised to buy beds made of red sandalwood before any other types of furniture. Indeed, just being in the museum should make us feel more youthful.

One of the nice and subtle touches is the background music, which is motion controlled so that it plays softly as one passes through the archway into another area. There are also cushioned stools and some comfortable chairs and sofas where one can rest and enjoy the surroundings.

How to get there:

Located just off the Jingtong Expressway very near the Gaobeidian exit.

京通高速公路高碑店出口处。

The Eastern Waterway

京东水道

The Grand Canal is a series of interconnected waterways in central and eastern China along which barges brought grain and other goods to the capital. Theoretically, the canal can still be navigated from Beijing all the way south to Guangzhou. In the Sụi Dynasty (581-618) it reached an area south of Beijing called Yuzhou, and was brought into the capital itself by a Yuan Dynasty (1271-1368) engineer and minister called Guo Shoujing.

In 1994, our group visited some sites on the waterway, starting with the first sluice gate, which is southeast of the China World Trade Center and across an east-west freight track. The sluice gate slowed the water's flow and raised its level to permit boats to pass into the canal proper. There is a stele here, expressing a welcome from the emperor, and carvings of four guardian water dragons.

The second sluice gate, farther east and within sight of the China Resources Hotel, was where wealthy people used to have picnics on the water in olden times. As a conduit for the capital's sewage, it has naturally lost its popularity.

Our next stop by the waterside was the Shifang Zhufo Baota, or Ten-Sided Precious Buddha Pagoda. This structure dates back to the days of Emperor Wanli (1573-1619) of the Ming Dynasty, and is all that remains of the Yanshousi, or Temple of Extended Life. The pagoda was restored in 1986.

Further on is the Yongtongqiao, or Ever-Flowing Bridge, which is unusual in that it has triple arches, permitting boats to pass without lowering their masts. Guo Shoujing erected the first bridge here, but the present one dates from 1446. It is built of stone, but has iron corner reinforcements, called "water slicers." The modern name is Baliqiao, or Eight-Li Bridge, and was the site of a battle in 1860 between the Anglo-French forces and Qing Dynasty troops.

We came to the village of Zhangjiawan. The waterway near here is the Yongding River. The village was a transfer point for grain until around 1800, when the river course

moved farther away from it. In the vicinity is a bridge called the Dashiqiao, said to be a better example of the 12th century Liao Dynasty style than the much-rebuilt Marco Polo Bridge.

Finally, we viewed from a distance the Randengta, or Light the Lamp Pagoda. It was erected in the Liao era, probably as a beacon tower, for this is where the northern part of the Grand Canal meets the Tonghui River.

How to get there:

In Chaoyang District.

朝阳区。

Liao-Jin City Wall Museum

北京辽金城垣博物馆

This museum is unique in that it is an actual archeological site. In 1990, a watergate was discovered which had been part of the city wall of Zhongdu, as Beijing was called when it was the capital city of the Jin Dynasty (1115-1234). The site was converted into a museum dedicated to the history of Beijing under the Jin and Liao (907-1125) dynasties, and opened to the public in 1995.

The watergate is considered to be a more intricate construction than those of later times. Visitors are taken underground to view the original wooden columns and layer of base stones; the rest of the site has been restored.

The first floor houses displays of artifacts and pictures relating to the period. In 1998, my daughter-in-law, Kosima Weber Liu, and her friend Ginny Anami held an exhibition here of photographs of temples and other historical sites around Beijing dating from the Liao and Jin dynasties.

How to get there:

Jia 40 Yulin Residential Quarter, Youanmenwai Dajie, Fengtai District.

丰台区右安门外大街玉林小区甲40号。

The Peking Opera School

北京市戏曲学校

The birth of Peking Opera is traditionally dated to 1790, when four local opera troupes from Anhui Province performed for the 80th birthday of Emperor Qianlong. Their various talents were synthesized thereafter, to produce the Peking Opera we know today and which is undergoing a revival after several decades of neglect by the public.

Traditional Chinese opera is characterized by a minimum of props and a great deal of symbolism. For instance, an actor holding a whip represents a man making a journey on horseback. The drama is expressed by means of costume, make-up, music and singing.

We were shown actors being made up in the four categories of *Sheng*, or male, *Dan*, or female, *Chou*, or clown, and *Jing*, or painted face, roles. Although facial colors are used for all roles, the *Jing* actors have the most extravagantly painted faces. The dominant colors tell the audience what kind of characters they are watching: Red signifies loyalty, black honesty, white treachery, blue refinement and elegance, and yellow cleverness. Gold and silver paint indicates that the actors are supernatural beings.

Actors playing *Sheng* roles fall into three categories: a man in his sixties, with a white beard and a weak voice, or in his fifties, with a grey beard; a younger man, with thicker make-up and a sing-song voice; and a warrior, with a natural voice. The *Dan* roles are divided into those of younger and older women, both expressing themselves in high-pitched voices. The *Chou* role involves humorous dialogue in natural tones, the white spot on the ridge of the nose showing humor and kind-heartedness. The *Jing* are all male roles, with booming voices.

Originally, all Peking Opera roles were played by men. After the fall of the Qing Dynasty in 1911, women began to mount the stage, although some traditional female roles continued to be performed by men. The late Mei Lanfang was the most outstanding actor of modern times in such parts.

The magnificent costumes are based on the styles

prevalent in the Ming Dynasty, no matter when the story is set. Emperors always wear orange robes decorated with golden dragons. Ministers wear red robes decorated with a dragon and a sun on top of a mountain, which signifies promotion. Robes which are split down the front, like riding coats, symbolize military attire or armor. We were shown an embroidered bridal costume that had taken 250 days to make.

Students come from all over the country to attend this school, starting their training at about eight years of age. After their first three years of basic training, they concentrate on a specific role. The strength and stamina required by Peking Opera roles are prodigious. We saw one young student do 30 back flips one after the other.

The Peking Opera School accepts qualified foreigners too. In 1992, I saw an English girl practicing the role of a woman general perfectly.

How to get there:

In the west of the South Third Ring Road, Fengtai District.

丰台区南三环西路。

Dabaotai Han Dynasty Tomb

北京大葆台西汉墓博物馆

This tomb, known as the Hanling, is located at Dabaotai, southwest of Beijing. It was excavated in 1974, and made into a museum in 1983. It is thought to have been the last resting place of Liu Jian (117-80 B.C.), ruler of the kingdom of Yan, a tributary state of the Han Dynasty.

The tomb was constructed entirely of wood, using no nails, and is the only example so far found of its type. The beams are clearly numbered, suggesting that it was designed and built first before being dismantled and re-assembled on the site. Layers of charcoal and plaster were placed above and below the wooden structure, to seal it against moisture. The occupant was buried in five coffins, one inside the other. This is an indication of high rank, but not as high as that of an emperor, who was buried in seven coffins. The inner coffin is made of Chinese catalpa wood, and the outer coffins are made of phellodendron wood.

The 400-odd objects found in the tomb include jade, lacquerware inlaid with gold plate and agate, finely woven and knotted silks, iron objects with the manufacturers' marks still visible, ceramics and terracotta tomb figures. Most remarkable are the three chariots and skeletons of 11 horses buried with the deceased. These chariots are the only known examples of Han Dynasty vehicles.

How to get there:

To the south of Guogongzhuang Village, Huaxiang in Fengtai District.

丰台区花乡郭公庄南。

The Marco Polo Bridge

卢沟桥

This bridge, the proper name of which is Lugouqiao, is mentioned in detail by Marco Polo in his book; hence the popular name. It spans the Yongding River, the major water source for Beijing in ancient times.

The first stone bridge was built here in 1189, by Emperor Shizong of the Jin Dynasty, using pillars of cedar wood. The riverbed is composed of treacherous mud and quicksand, and the river is notorious for flooding. As a consequence, the bridge was destroyed several times. The original bridge is now preserved as a cultural relic, and the river is now crossed by a brand-new one built a few yards away in 1987. The bridge is intricately carved, mainly with figures of lions, and marble elephants support each end of it. When we visited it, the bridge was being used as a backdrop for a historical movie.

Lugouqiao has played an important role in Chinese history: It was here that Jin troops mutinied and opened up the road to the capital for Genghis Khan; and a clash between Chinese and Japanese troops here on July 7, 1937, sparked the all-out War of Resistance to Japanese Aggression.

How to get there:

In the west of Fengtai District.

丰台区西部。

The Fahai Temple

法海寺

Located on Mount Cuiwei, on the western outskirts of Beijing, this temple is famous for its Buddhist murals. The temple was built with funds collected by the Ming court eunuch Li Tong. It was begun in 1439, and completed in four years.

The murals, covering 236.7 sq m, are in the Daxiong Hall, the only surviving building. Traditional Chinese painting techniques were used to depict more than 70 images of Buddha, deities and fairies, including the Boddhisatvas of water and the moon. The colors are still bright. An inscription on a stone pillar records that the murals were painted by court painters of the Ming Dynasty.

Two lacebark pines planted at the time of the construction of the temple are still flourishing in front of the hall.

How to get there:

In Moshikou, Shijingshan District.

石景山区模式口。

Museum of Traces of the Ice Age

中国第四纪冰川遗迹陈列馆

Striations in rocks in the vicinity led to the setting up of this museum. The traces are evidence of movements of glaciers during the Fourth Ice Age, and were identified by Li Siguang, one of modern China's most famous geologists. Li discovered the deposits at Daqing, China's largest oilfield, proving that China did indeed have vast oil reserves. Li was responsible for the museum, and there is a bust of him in the courtyard.

In 1996, the 30th World Geological Congress was held in Beijing, when experts from 29 countries visited the museum. The exhibits include minerals and fossils, as well as glacier-scratched rocks.

How to get there:

28 Moshikou, Shijingshan District.

石景山区模式口28号院。

The Eunuch's Tomb

田义墓

Tian Yi Mu, or the Tomb of Tian Yi, is not far from the Museum of Traces of the Ice Age. It was opened to the public in 1988, bringing the number of Beijing museums to 101.

Visitors are given an explanation of the institution of eunuchs as imperial servants. Many were castrated as small children and sold to the court by their parents. Often, prisoners of war were made eunuchs; others were made so as punishment for misdeeds. It was not unusual for a eunuch to rise to very high rank, or even to dominate the court and acquire fabulous riches.

Tian Yi's title was Master of the Seal, in charge of rituals. He also supervised the supply of spirits, vinegar and flour for the imperial household. The tomb was robbed repeatedly over the years, and now only two pieces of the coffin are left in the tomb chamber, which can be entered by visitors. In the back courtyard, or *Yinzhai*, where the tombs are, there is a complete set of five stone sacrificial vessels and a sacrificial table with drawers carved in it. These are only symbolic, because the actual rituals for the dead were carried out in the front courtyard, or *Yangzhai*.

How to get there:

Moshikou Dajie, Shijingshan District.

石景山区模式口大街。

Badachu

八大处公园

The name Badachu refers to the "Eight Great Temples" situated in a compact area known as Cuiwei Hill in the Western Hills. It is a favorite spot for weekend outings, especially when temple fairs are being held. The temples themselves have their own unique features and are well worth visiting.

At the foot of the hill is the Temple of Eternal Peace. It was constructed in 1504, during the Ming Dynasty. In one of the two main halls is a statue of Guan Yu, a hero of the Three Kingdoms Period (220-280) who later became deified as the God of War and worshipped as a temple guardian. There is also a bronze bell cast in 1600 by imperial command. In the rear courtyard are two white pine trees known as dragon-claw pines, reputed to date from the Yuan Dynasty.

A little farther up the hill is the Temple of Divine Light. This temple was destroyed during the Boxer Movement of 1900, and only the fishpond and the Foundation of the Pagoda for Entertaining Immortals are left of the original structure. After the destruction of the temple, monks searching the rubble came across a wooden box containing a tooth. The box was inside a stone chest, upon which the words "Tooth of Sakyamuni" were carved, together with the date 855 and the name of a monk, Shan Hui. In 1956, the government erected a 13-story pagoda to house the tooth. Some nearby buildings were restored and a visitors' center set up.

The next stop is at the Three Hills Convent, which gets its name because it is situated between Cuiwei, Pingpo and Lushi hills. At the doorway of the main hall is a traditional rectangular "cloud and water stone," carved with images of scenery, human figures and animals.

The three main halls in the Temple of Great Compassion date from different periods of the Ming Dynasty. One of the courtyards is thickly planted with a rare type of bamboo which remains green all winter. There are two huge gingko trees reputed to be over 800 years old.

The Dragon King Temple is also known as the Dragon Spring Convent. It was built in the early years of the Qing Dynasty. A spring bubbles up from a cliff behind the second courtyard and flows through both courtyards and out of a stone spigot carved in the shape of a dragon's head. The water is said to never freeze in winter.

The largest temple complex at Badachu is the Temple of the Fragrant World. It was once an imperial summer retreat. The temple's Sojourn Palace and Scripture Repository were erect-ed by Emperor Qianlong. Cuiwei Hill gets its name from a Ming princess who is buried here.

Behind a memorial archway is the Precious Pearl Temple. This is situated on the summit of the hill, and affords a panoramic view of Beijing, with Kunming Lake to the east, the Yongding River to the southwest, the plains to the south and the city skyline in the center. The temple's name comes from a cavern behind the main hall and a stone near its mouth which resembles a large pearl.

On Lushi Hill, named after a monk who is said to have traveled all the way from southern China in a rowboat, stands the oldest structure at Badachu, the Temple of Buddhahood, also known as the Temple of Pacifying the Nation. This temple was built about 1,200 years ago. The courtyard contains exquisitely wrought rockeries, and in front of the main hall is a stone tablet and a two-meter-high bronze bell.

How to get there:

In the north of Shijingshan District.

石景山区北部。

The Ordination Temple

戒台寺

This temple, the Jietaisi, lies in the Ma'an Mountains, some 35 km to the west of Beijing. It was built in 622, at the beginning of the Tang Dynasty, and named Huiju. In the 11th century, Abbott Fajun built a terrace for the ordination of monks. The temple attracted great numbers of novices for ordination, and so became known as the Jietaisi, or Ordination Temple. The temple is composed of several compounds, with the halls of Heavenly Kings, Thousand Buddhas, Three Immortals and Nine Immortals running from west to east. There are also the Jietai Compound, the Peony compound, and monks' living quarters.

The Ordination Temple is famous for its ancient pine trees, one of which is the Inclining Dragon Pine, with its roots deep in a stone wall and its branches spreading horizontally, giving it the appearance of flying dragon. There is also the "Trembling Pine," so called because if you pull any of its branches the whole structure of branches and leaves will move. Some 200 years ago, Emperor Qianlong wrote a poem in honor of this tree, and there is a stele in the temple grounds bearing the words of the poem.

How to get there:

In Mentougou District, 35 kilometers from the downtown Beijing.

门头沟区，距市区 35 公里。

A Ming Dynasty Village

川底下古建山庄

West of Beijing and past the coal mines of Mentougou, there is a village which has changed little since it was founded in Ming times. The 104 original families had moved up into the mountains to escape warfare in the plains.

In 1994, when our group visited it, the village was home to 20 families, all surnamed Han and totaling 40-50 people. Many of the houses are still furnished in Ming style, and the old North China *kang* (heated brick bed) is very much in evidence. The old landlord's house preserves some fancy carvings.

Returning in 1996, we found that the villagers were making efforts to attract tourists. There is a small museum displaying ancient tools and artifacts, and a tea shop.

How to get there:

In Mentougou District.

门头沟区。

Mentougou

门头沟

This small township is the place where a lot of the coal for the city of Beijing is mined. A cut was made through the mountains for a road on which to transport it, and in early times camels pulled carts loaded with coal into the city through a special gate.

Later, a railway line was built for the coal. The line also served to transport sightseers to the nearby temples in the Western Hills.

There is a village called Liulichu in Mentougou, which used to provide all the glazed tiles for the whole of China. They still make glazed tiles, but there are also factories in other parts of the country now. It is easy to find a tile factory in the area. The people there will be happy to show you around and sell you samples.

There is a pavilion straddling the road, which Emperor Qianlong used to visit. It can only be viewed from the outside as yet. The local people told us there are several other historic spots nearby, but as there is no money to renovate them they remain neglected and unvisited.

How to get there:

In the west of Beijing.

北京西部。

Xihaizi Park

西海子公园

The main attraction of this park is a Tang Dynasty pagoda with a chequered history. It was destroyed by the Tangshan earthquake in 1976, but rebuilt in 1987. It has 13 stories, making it 56 meters high. From each story hang 184 bells–2,288 altogether–each bell bearing the name of its contributor. A bone relic of the Buddha is said to have been preserved here throughout the vicissitudes of the centuries. The approach to the pagoda is lined with animal figures which were originally the guardians of the "spirit road" to the tomb of a Ming Dynasty empress.

The pagoda was a stop on the Grand Canal for boats taking tribute rice and wheat to Beijing. Behind it is a small temple with a statue of Sakyamuni. In the courtyard is a tree said to date from the Han Dynasty, and a Ming Dynasty stele mounted on a stone turtle.

Also in the park is the tomb of Li Jiuwu, a Ming Dynasty writer and historian. He was the same sort of revolutionary literary figure in his day as Lu Xun was in the early 20th century. In fact, he provoked so much official opprobrium that he was executed by order of the emperor.

How to get there:

In Tongxian County.

北京通县。

The Hongluo Temple

红螺寺

This temple is located in Huairou County, 57 km from downtown Beijing. It was built in 348, during the Eastern Jin Dynasty. Its original name was Daming (Great Light), and its present name, Hongluo (Red Conch Shell), derives from a local legend which held that in ancient times there were two conch shells in the pond behind the temple, which emitted a mysterious red light. Hongluo is also the name of the mountain to the rear of the temple.

There are five compounds, including those containing the Heavenly King Hall, the Great Hero Hall and the Three Sages Hall, and an area containing stupas, in which the remains of eminent monks are enshrined. There are also guest rooms and quarters for both practicing and retired monks.

The Hongluo Temple was famous as a place for teaching *qigong* (a set of traditional physical exercises including breath control).

Outside the Great Hero Hall are two gingko trees which are 1,000 years old and 30 meters tall. The female tree does not bloom, but bears fruit in autumn; the male tree blooms in spring, but does not bear fruit.

One of the temple's most illustrious inhabitants was the High Monk Jixing (1741-1810), who was the 12th master of the Pure Land sect of Buddhism. His stupa contains his granulated ashes and some of his teeth.

How to get there:

Located in Huairou County, 57 km from downtown Beijing.

怀柔县境内，距北京市区 57 公里。

The Silver Mountain Pagoda Forest

银山塔林风景区

At one time there were 72 Buddhist shrines on Silver Mountain, at Changping, to the west of the Ming Tombs, cared for by 500 monks. But all that remain now are abandoned pagodas and stupas, the two upright stones which held the flagstaff of the temple complex, a well and the base of an altar. Some restoration work is being done.

Pagodas were built for three purposes: as burial places for monks, to improve the auspiciousness of the surroundings according to the principles of geomancy, and as places of worship.

At Silver Mountain there are examples of very tall pagodas with highly decorative designs. The five pagodas dating from the Jin Dynasty contain the remains of important monks, the most famous being Fo Jue. High on the hillside is a pagoda built in memory of a renowned monk who once preached there. It is said that walking around this pagoda three times clockwise and three times counter-clockwise will cure back pain. Nearby is the Cave Facing the Sun, where a hermit once lived.

Our group visited Silver Mountain in 1995, and had an enjoyable time exploring the relics of bygone days tucked into valleys and woods and beside little water courses.

How to get there:

In the north of Changping County.

昌平县北部。

The Cloud Terrace

云台

This edifice at the Juyong Pass, near the Great Wall at Badaling, is a beautifully carved white marble archway. It was built in the latter years of the Yuan Dynasty. It has a balustrade consisting of 55 pillars adorned with carvings of stylized flames. On the top is an image of Garuda, a being from Hindu mythology half man and half bird, welcoming people to what used to be the most important northern gateway to Beijing.

We first visited the Cloud Terrace in 1990, at which time it dominated the landscape and the nearby sections of the Great Wall were in ruins. When we returned in 1998, we found to our chagrin that it was in the middle of a parking lot and was dwarfed by renovations that had been done to the wall.

How to get there:

Located at the Juyong Pass in the Yanqing County, northeast of Beijing.

北京东北地区延庆县居庸关。

Yanqing County Cave Dwellings

延庆县古崖居遗址

These mysterious excavations, although they are said to date from the eighth century, only came to the attention of archeologists about 20 years ago. There are about 150 caves carved out of the mountainsides in Yanqing County, not far from the Guanting Reservoir.

Our group scrambled up and down exploring the various

doorways, niches and hewn steps. Some of the caves appear to have been stables, as they have what look like feeding troughs along one wall. A few were of several stories, with holes in the floors and ceilings for access by ladder.

Legend has it that the caves were the homes of the Xi people, a group of fugitive slaves during the Tang Dynasty, yet the absence of carvings, inscriptions and artifacts of any kind hinders further study of the cave dwellers.

How to get there:

In Zhangshanying Village, 15 km west of Yanqing County.

延庆县西部15公里张山营乡。

Dragon Gorge, or Longqingxia

龙庆峡

This spectacular canyon, Longqingxia, surrounded by imposing peaks, is called the "Guilin of the north," after the famous scenic spot in south China. The river is dammed, and a series of escalators takes visitors to the top of the dam, from where they board boats for a trip along the winding Longqing River.

The way is signposted with Monkey King figures, and statues of cranes and a large Buddha figure have also been erected. Leaving the boat at a temple, tourists can scramble up the surrounding hills to viewing pavilions, buy souvenirs and watch high-wire stunts. It is also possible to rent a rowboat and explore the river on your own.

Returning to the starting point, the passengers are let off and descend through a tunnel. For the fearless, it is also possible to hurtle down a specially built track on a go-cart.

How to get there:

15 km northeast of the Yanqing County, 80 km from downtown Beijing.

延庆县城东北 15 公里处，距市区 80 公里。

Mount Shangfang National Forest Park

上方山国家森林公园

The forest park is in rugged mountainous terrain some 62 km southwest of Beijing, in the suburban district of Fangshan. It is home to more than 625 varieties of wild plants, all of them protected. In addition, there are more than 200 ancient trees, one of which is a cypress said to be over 1,500 years old, standing beside the Luzhou Pavilion.

Besides cypresses, there are pines, ginkgoes and Chinese scholartrees, as well as winter sweets, lilacs and bauhinias. In 1994, the park was designated as one of 20 model forest parks in China.

Mount Shangfang has been a favorite retreat for Buddhists since about the year 58, and by the Ming Dynasty there were at least 70 monasteries there. Nowadays, only 17 are well preserved. The largest one, the Doushai Monastery, was built during the Sui Dynasty. It was restored in 1985, in Ming architectural style. In the grounds are more than 50 ancient tombs, including some cave tombs, and epitaphs.

The summit of the mountain, 800 meters above sea level, is attained by a *yunti*, or "Cloud Ladder"–262 stone steps. Climbers are protected along the steep spiral path by a thick chain. At the top is the Cloud Ladder Pavilion, which affords a magnificent view of the surrounding countryside. On the southern slope of the mountain is the Yunshui (Cloud Water) Cave, containing a sculptured Buddha done in the Liao Dynasty. The 620-meter-long cave contains seven chambers open to tourists. The largest chamber has a floor space of 2,000 sq meters. The cave boasts the tallest stalagmite so far discovered in China–38 meters. It has been identified as being 350,000 years old.

We visited the park in 1998, and found the tour very strenuous but well worth the effort. It is fairly isolated, so it is not commercialized or crowded.

How to get there:

In Yuegezhuang Village, Fangshan District, some 62 km southwest of Beijing.

房山区岳各庄，北京西南约62公里。

The Yunju Temple

云居寺

This temple is located in Fangshan County, about 75 km southwest of downtown Beijing and on the western side of Mount Shijing. It was built in the Sui Dynasty (581-618), and often expanded in later dynasties. The original temple had six main halls, arranged from east to west. Most of the buildings were destroyed during the fighting against the Japanese invaders in the 1930s.

The temple is famous for its collection of Buddhist scriptures carved on stone slabs. The work began in 605, and now there are altogether 14,278 slabs. They are stored in the basement of the Scripture Pagoda and in the nine caves of the Stone Scripture Hill, east of the temple. Two pagodas used to stand on the northern and southern sides of the temple, but only the northern one, first built in 711, remains.

In 1992, the Yunju Temple was selected as one of the top ten tourists spots in the Beijing area by the municipal government.

How to get there:

In Changgou Village, Fangshan District.

房山区长沟乡。

Temple of Solitary Happiness

独乐寺

The Temple of Solitary Happiness (Dulesi) is located in the town of Jixian, about 100 km east of Beijing. The original temple was built in the Sui Dynasty, and rebuilt in the Tang and Liao dynasties. Three stories high, the temple is the oldest multi-storied building in North China, and is constructed in such an ingenious way that it has survived 20 earthquakes.

We visited the temple in 1993, just before it was to be closed for a lengthy period of renovations, and were able to ascend to the gallery to view the head of a magnificent 16-meter-high statue of Guanyin, the Goddess of Mercy, which is the temple's main feature.

The surrounding halls contain murals on religious and folklore themes, painted in the Liao, Yuan and Ming dynasties. The nearby White Pagoda, built in 1058, was originally part of the temple complex.

How to get there:

In Jixian County, Tianjin.

天津蓟县境内。

The Huangya Pass

黄崖关长城

The Huangya (Yellow Cliff) Pass on the Great Wall is located where the Ju River cuts through the hills north of Beijing. This section of the wall was constructed by the Ming general Qi Jiguang, and there is a military camp "city" attached to it.

The camp is divided into three parts: the Outer Gate Area, the City Proper and what was once the Inner City, closest to the hills. Unlike the imperial cities, which were laid out on a strict grid pattern, military cities were built for defense, so the streets were labyrinthine. A training ground was located in the hills.

Inside the Tidiaoyamen (Keeper of the Keys Office), decorated with black lacquer trimmed with red, is a museum showing the layout of the former encampment. On display also are ancient grenades and a bronze cannon. There is a statue in the courtyard of a young Mao Zedong.

The fort hosts the annual September Mountain Products Fair.

How to get there:

In Jixian County, Tianjin.

天津蓟县。

The Eastern Qing Tombs

清东陵

Located 125 km northeast of Beijing, the Eastern Qing Tombs (Qingdongling), like the Western Qing Tombs, are the burial grounds of Qing Dynasty emperors, empresses and imperial concubines. The area is about 25 sq km.

Traditionally, great care was taken in choosing a tomb site, as this was supposed to affect the prosperity or otherwise of one's descendants. The art of geomancy, or *fengshui*, was highly revered and used for picking one's last resting place. The Eastern Qing Tombs are reckoned to have perfect *fengshui*, which protects them from natural disasters. Indeed, when an earthquake measuring 7.8 on the Richter scale hit Tangshan, less than 100 km away, in 1976, the tomb area was unaffected, even though the quake toppled buildings as far away as in Beijing.

Construction of the first tomb was begun in the second year of the reign of Emperor Kangxi (1663), and the area contains the mausoleums of the following emperors: Shunzhi (1644-1661), Kangxi (1662-1722), Qianlong (1736-1796), Xianfeng (1851-1861) and Tongzhi (1862-1875). The most remarkable one is that of Empress Dowager Cixi (1835-1908). In addition, there are the tombs of 14 empresses, 136 imperial concubines and several princesses.

The tombs of Qianlong and Cixi have been renovated, and are open to the public. Cixi was co-regent with another empress dowager,

Ci'an, and their tombs, as was the custom, were prepared during their lifetimes at the same time and in the same style. Cixi, however, was not satisfied with her "accommodation,"

and had it rebuilt at enormous expense.

In 1928, the warlord Sun Dianying, on the pretext of using the area for military maneuvers, plundered the mausoleums of both Qianlong and Cixi. It is said that 25,000 pearls, 200 pieces of jade and 80 gems were stolen from Cixi's coffin, as well as a priceless luminous pearl placed in her mouth.

Objects left behind by the looters can be viewed in an exhibition hall in Cixi's mausoleum. They include the Empress Dowager's clothing and burial garments, paintings and articles of daily use.

How to get there:

In Zunhua County, Hebei Province.

河北遵化。

The Western Qing Tombs

清西陵

The Western Tombs of the Qing Dynasty lie at the foot of Mount Yongning in Yixian County, Hebei Province. Here are located the stately mausoleums of emperors Yongzheng (1723-1736), Jiaqing (1796-1821), Daoguang (1821-1851) and Guangxu (1875-1908), together with the tombs of three empresses, seven princes and a number of imperial concubines.

Since 1997, they have been joined by the not-so-stately tomb of the last emperor, Puyi. The latter ruled from 1909 to 1911, with the reign title Xuantong, and was forced to abdicate following the 1911 Revolution.

The first mausoleum to be constructed here (Tailing) was that of the third Qing emperor, Yongzheng. Work began in 1730, and lasted seven years. The Tailing is the largest of the Western Tombs, and occupies the central position. It is approached by the broad Sacred Way, lined with pines and cypresses. Just inside the Great Red Gate, which is the main entrance to the whole area, is the Dressing Hall, where the principal worshipper, usually the deceased emperor's eldest surviving son, would change into ceremonial robes before performing the ancestral rites. Passing over a seven-arch stone bridge, the Sacred Way is then flanked by ten pairs of stone sculptures, six of animals and two each of civil and military officials.

To the west of the Tailing is the Changling of Emperor Jiaqing. The two complexes are nearly identical in terms of the number of buildings and style of architecture and decoration. In accordance with Qing Dynasty practice, Empress Xiaosurui, who predeceased Jiaqing, was buried in the Changling, but her successor, who died after the demise of the emperor, was buried in a separate tomb.

Five km to the west of the Changling is the tomb of Emperor Daoguang, the Muling. Daoguang originally had a tomb constructed for himself at the Eastern site, but shifted it to the Western Tombs when seepage of water into the tomb chamber was blamed on dragons angry at some *fengshui* blunder.

To the east of the Tailing is the mausoleum of Emperor Guangxu, the Chongling. It was begun posthumously in 1909, and was left unfinished by the fall of the Qing Dynasty two years later. The Republican government provided funds for its completion in 1915. Nearby is the tomb of Guangxu's concubines Zhenfei and her sister Jinfei. The jealous Empress Dowager Cixi ordered her chief eunuch Cui Yugui to murder Zhenfei, which he did by throwing her down a well.

Acres of pines, cypresses and fruit trees have been planted here, making it an ideal place for picnics, with peach and plum trees blossoming in the spring and apple and persimmon trees blooming in the autumn.

How to get there:

In Yixian County, Hebei Province.

河北易县。

Bibliography

Ancient Temple in Beijing, published by China Esperanto Press, 1993.

Beijing Old and New, Zhou Shachen New World Press, 1984.

Beijing-China's Ancient and Modern Capital, Liu Junwen, Foreign Language Press, Beijing, 1982.

In Search of Old Peking, L.C. Arlington Nagel's Encyclopedia of China, pub. 1958, Nagel Publishers, Geneva, Switzerland.

Rain Flower Pebbles, edited by Zuo Heng and Wu Mingchi, Jiangsu People's Publishing House, 1990.

图书在版编目（CIP）数据

北京自助游：英文／（美）刘爱伦（Liu, E.）编著
北京：外文出版社，2000.12

ISBN 7-119-02001-3
Ⅰ.北… Ⅱ.刘… Ⅲ.旅游指南—北京市—英文 Ⅳ.K928.91
中国版本图书馆 CIP 数据核字（2000）第 76538 号

责任编辑 赵优
美术编辑 陈军

外文出版社网页：
http://www.flp.com.cn
外文出版社电子邮件地址：
info@flp.com.cn
sales@flp.com.cn

北京自助游

Eleanor Liu 著

*

外文出版社

外文出版社出版

（中国北京百万庄大街 24 号）

邮政编码 100037

中国国际图书贸易总公司发行

（中国北京车公庄西路 35 号）

北京邮政信箱第 399 号 邮政编码 100044

2001 年（36 开）第 1 版

2001 年第 1 版第 1 次印刷

（英）

ISBN 7-119-02001-3/G·365（外）

03000（平）

17-E-3424P